D0098733

RUDE

STOP
Being Nice
AND
START
Being Bold

REBECCA REID

Simon & Schuster

New York London Toronto Sydney New Delhi

Simon & Schuster
1230 Avenue of the Americas
New York, NY 10020

Originally published in Great Britain in 2020
by Trapeze as *The Power of Rude*

This Simon & Schuster hardcover edition December 2020

SIMON & SCHUSTER and colophon are registered
trademarks of Simon & Schuster, Inc.

For information about special discounts for bulk purchases,
please contact Simon & Schuster Special Sales at
1-866-506-1949 or business@simonandschuster.com.

The Simon & Schuster Speakers Bureau can bring authors
to your live event. For more information or to book an event,
contact the Simon & Schuster Speakers Bureau at
1-866-248-3049 or visit our website at www.simonspeakers.com.

Interior design by Lewelin Polanco

Manufactured in the United States of America

1 3 5 7 9 10 8 6 4 2

Library of Congress Cataloging-in-Publication
Data has been applied for.

ISBN 978-1-9821-4082-3
ISBN 978-1-9821-4084-7 (ebook)

This book is dedicated to me,
because I wrote it.

And Lucy,
because she really
needs to read it.

Contents

Contents

A Note on Language

Rude is based around my experiences and the experiences of the women whom I interviewed for the book, who were predominantly straight or bisexual. So when the book addresses romantic relationships, it tends to assume that the couple is a man and a woman.

This is not to suggest that heterosexual relationships are the "right" or "normal" types of relationships, just that they are the most common and therefore what most women experience. In addition, most studies show that gay women report higher relationship satisfaction and have more fulfilling sex lives than women in heterosexual relationships; the advice in the dating and sex chapters really is mostly for straight women, who are much more in need of it. If you're not having sex with men, skip the sex and dating chapters and reflect on how enormously lucky you are.

Finally, in writing the book, I opted not to use "women and nonbinary people" and "women in heterosexual relationships" simply to avoid clunkiness. Using standardized language throughout the book was intended for simplicity and ease of readership, not erasure.

Methodology

In order to gather as much information about the relationship between women and rudeness as possible, I put together an anonymous survey, which invited women to answer specific yes-or-no questions and to add comments of unlimited length. One hundred fifty-two women took part.

The survey was shared widely outside my own networks, but I wanted to make sure that I wasn't just representing people from my age group or location. I interviewed a variety of women who were forty or older, as the majority of the respondents to the survey were under forty.

I also spent a lot of time sitting in cafés and riding on buses, listening to women talk to each other. As a naturally nosy person, I found this perfectly normal, but other people have expressed horror at this method. It was, however, enormously useful in terms of observing the dynamics between other women, as well as testing my hypothesis that women from all backgrounds and of all ages worry about seeming rude on a daily basis.

RUDE

Have You Ever?

- Paid in full for a terrible meal.
- Lain awake while your neighbors played their music full blast.
- Taken the stairs at double speed because someone was behind you.
- Pretended to forget that a friend owes you money.
- Kept a gift you hated instead of asking for the receipt.
- Pretended to be in a relationship to avoid a flirty stranger.
- Laughed along with a joke that really hurt your feelings.
- Put away someone else's equipment at the end of a gym class.
- Stayed silent when someone jumped a line you were waiting in.
- Kept your seat upright on a flight while the person in front of you was fully reclined.
- Let your friend bring a boyfriend to a girls' night.
- Routinely cleaned up after your housemate.

If you've done, or regularly do, any of the above, then you've come to exactly the right place.

These may seem like small things, and in isolation they are. But if you do a handful of these little things each week out of a desire to avoid being rude, by the end of the month or the year, the list of ways that you have twisted yourself around other people's wants and needs is a mile long. *Rude* will teach you to step outside of that behavior.

The last hundred years has seen incredible progress for women, and in terms of the rights we have enshrined in law, things look better than ever. Never has feminism been more popular, widespread, or well represented. Emma Watson, Beyoncé, Taylor Swift—the vast majority of famous women identify as feminists. People like me make a living out of being feminist. And yet despite all that, women all over the world continue to experience sexism day in and day out.

The pay gap endures, reproductive freedom is under attack, sexual violence abounds, maternity rights and childcare provisions still lock women out of the workplace. Many of the world's most powerful nations have still never had a female leader. So, despite what you might see on tote bags and pink pencils, necklaces and T-shirts, feminism isn't finished. The war for women is not won.

It is important to keep fighting for societal change. But that type of change is slow and difficult to bring about. And the unfair reality is that the responsibility of improving the system that oppresses women most often falls to women. If we want to continue the feminist revolution that was started by the suffragettes, then, in addition to fighting for societal change, we also need to tackle the expectations that, as individuals, we conform to—often without really meaning to. I'm talking about the expectation that women will smile sweetly, sit nicely, take up as little space as possible, and put their own wants and needs last for fear of seeming rude.

When I started writing *Rude*, I decided to keep a diary noting down the times I did something because I didn't want to be rude. I thought I would need to keep it for several weeks in order to notice much, but from the very first day, the issue was clear.

TUESDAY

8:30 a.m.
I wake up and realize that I didn't set my alarm. I'm running late, so I call a taxi to take me to work, which cuts the journey time in half.

9:00 a.m.
I get into the taxi. It's way too hot, but the driver seems to like it this way, so I start stripping off layers. I consider opening the window but decide against it. He puts the radio on to a noisy sports game. I have a headache but assume this is some kind of important match that he would be sad to miss, so again I say nothing.

When I arrive at my office, where I work as the digital editor of a women's magazine, I feel embarrassed about having taken a taxi and hope no one sees.

9:30 a.m.
If I buy a coffee, I will be four minutes late to the office but much more productive. I don't have the balls to nonchalantly

3

roll in late, so I skip the coffee. I am sleepy through my next two meetings as a result.

10:15 a.m.

One of the writers I edit files a piece that hasn't really hit the mark, but I like her too much to say anything, so I rewrite it myself.

1:00 p.m.

Lunch! Earlier in the week I batch-cooked a curry and a soup. My husband asked which one I wanted. I claimed I didn't care either way, even though I did, and have ended up with the soup. I curse myself as I plow through it.

2:30 p.m.

One of the team members whom I technically manage (though I have a strong tendency toward the Regina George's Mom School of Management) takes ninety minutes for lunch. When she comes back, I say, "Everything okay?" which is designed to be a code for "Why are you so late?" "Everything's fine!" she says with a smile.

5:30 p.m.

I have finished all of the things that I need to do for the day and come to a natural conclusion. I could easily go home, but I'm worried someone will notice and think that I'm lazy, so instead I browse ASOS and think about getting bangs. At six p.m., which is when our day is supposed to finish, I stand around making noises about being "kind of done" until people start telling me I should leave.

7:30 p.m.

I take the same ballet class every week. I arrive early to claim my favorite spot. Another woman arrives late and stands inexplicably close to me. I'm in danger of accidentally kicking her, so I give up my spot and move down the barre.

9:00 p.m.

I'm home from ballet and I need to wash my hair, but my husband hasn't made dinner (he's not one of life's cooks—and he does all the dishes), so I end up roasting eggplants and plan to get up earlier and wash my hair tomorrow, which will inevitably mean I am late.

11:00 p.m.

I'm just falling asleep as my husband starts to snore like a buzz saw. I consider sleeping elsewhere but then decide sleeping apart would mean I am a bad wife. Rather than wake him up, I wait until I'm seething with anger and exhaustion, then I snap and pull the duvet off him. He wakes up looking hurt and sad. I feel hideously guilty and apologize. He goes back to sleep. I listen to him snore.

No one likes homework. But in order to get the most out of this book, I would encourage you to keep a diary for a day or a week and to be completely honest with yourself about each moment during the day that has been dictated by your fear of seeming rude.

Rude: The Definition

RUDE (adjective): Offensively impolite or bad mannered

"She had been rude to her boss."
"He is a rude and arrogant bully."

It's just before seven in the morning and I'm standing in a TV studio, about to go on breakfast television. This is normal—this is part of my job. As a journalist and feminist commentator, I'm regularly offered a seat at a desk or on a sofa so I can, to put it bluntly, have a fight with Piers Morgan.

The format is almost always the same. I arrive at the studio, often still half-asleep; get my hair and makeup done, which function like a kind of armor; and chug a cup of coffee. After an extensive and nuanced research chat, I then get on set and have a much less nuanced and much angrier debate with someone who has been cast because they have the exact opposite opinion from mine. I'll usually have Piers Morgan shouting from one side and the fellow panelist shouting on the other.

Today I'm nervous. The person who is attaching a microphone to my bra has cold hands. Incidentally, microphones—

they go in your jacket pocket if you're a man, but if you wear a dress on TV, that means you're getting a cold hand down your back while an embarrassed sound technician tries to make the mic pack clip onto your underwear.

I don't usually get nervous, but today I'm tired and stressed. It's early in the morning and I've gained a little weight in the run-up to Christmas, which means there'll be even more horrible comments on social media as soon as we're done. Plus, it's a divisive topic: should there be limits on what jokes comedians can make?

The producers shepherd me down a corridor and introduce me to my fellow guest, a comedian who was told he couldn't make sexist or racist jokes at a charity event and caused a small news story by objecting to the order. "Hi," I say with a smile, offering my hand. "It's nice to meet you." He smiles back, perfectly friendly, just like they always are.

TV producers like to keep debate guests in different rooms before the show. They do this for two reasons: because they don't want you to get into the debate off camera, and because it's much harder to have a fiery debate with someone if you've made friends in the greenroom. More on that later.

Anyway, they point us in the right direction and tell the comedian to stand in front of me. "Shouldn't it be ladies first?" He smirks. "Oh wait, is that sexist?"

I smile, perhaps roll my eyes a little, but say nothing. He is trying to wind me up. It works, but I don't acknowledge it. You see, I'm a nice girl. I keep cool when people try to bait me with lazy jokes about sexism. I'm here for a debate, but I still want everyone to like me. This—I am about to realize—has always been my mistake.

Minutes later we're on air and I'm asked a question. The comedian has already had his say, and now he's trying to talk over me. Before I realize what I'm doing, I put my finger to my lips and I shush him, like I would if he were a naughty child. I keep shushing him, and when he continues talking I say: "Either I can talk, or we can both talk, but I'm not going to stop talking." And he stops.

For the first time in as long as I can remember, a man has stopped talking to let me have my say. And it feels incredible, like I've shattered my own personal glass ceiling. After years of fighting to be heard at dinner parties and work meetings, I have finally snapped and thrown my full force at the problem.

The interview finishes and we make friendly noises toward each other, shake hands, and part amicably. Then, almost immediately, everything explodes. Social media lights up with horror at my behavior. I am dubbed "Rebecca Rude." I am briefly a news story. I go home for Christmas and distant family members think it's funny to put their finger to their mouth and shush me as a greeting (it is quite funny actually). Overnight I have become known as a Rude Woman.

Initially I'm mortified. I am not rude. At least, not in the traditional sense. I've been complimented on my manners since I was a small child. I always say please and thank you. I tip, I send birthday cards, I don't complain about splitting the bill even if I only had a main course. I used to write a column about etiquette and I pen a heck of a thank-you letter.

But the longer it goes on, the more people call me "Rebecca Rude," the more I start to realize: the last decade of my life has been a journey to deprogram myself. A mission to unlearn the messages I was taught as a child and teenager. With every year that passes, I become ruder. And it is no coincidence that the ruder I get, the happier and more successful I become.

Rudeness, I realize, is a talent. And rather than shying away from it, I'm going to turn it into my own personal superpower.

What Does It Really Mean to Be Rude?

If we're going to talk about rudeness for an entire book, then we should probably understand what we mean by the word.

The kind of rudeness that this book defends is what I'd term "positive rudeness." It is, to be totally honest, the kind of behavior that is called "rude" when it comes from a woman and "assertive" when it comes from a man. Positive rudeness means politely saying you'd prefer not to pay for food that is inedible. Plain old-fashioned (unacceptable) rudeness means insulting the chef or taking out your rage on the waitstaff, who are probably tired, bored, and on minimum wage, and had nothing to do with the preparation of said food.

Positive rudeness is about judging that your wants and needs are at least as important as everyone else's and then acting accordingly.

If you're looking for justification for yelling at your cleaning lady or cutting someone off when you're driving, then you are, to coin a phrase, shit out of luck. What this book is going to do is show you what life looks like when you stop worrying about the idea that you might seem rude.

It's Not (Always) Easy, Being Rude

I won't lie: on my path to rebalance my levels of rudeness, I have sometimes gotten it wrong. Having spent my entire life trying to avoid rudeness, it was—and sometimes still is—a challenge to deploy the right amount of it at the right time. Take, for example, my rude epiphany on national breakfast television. Just after the shushing, I said, "You've had your chance to speak and now I am going to have mine." A sentence that every woman should have in her arsenal. Only, no one was particularly interested in that part. What people cared about was the shush, which was possibly a little bit on the childish side. It felt good, though.

Creating the perfect cocktail of rude is a challenge. I've sent an email or two to someone senior to me that was too rude. Honest, accurate, and probably fair, but not the best way to get the reaction I wanted. Similarly, I have approached debates at parties with a ferocity that would have been more appropriate for a boardroom takeover than for cocktails. Skewering a friend's date because he gets the numbers wrong when he cites the 2017 election might win the argument, but it doesn't get you a lot of repeat invitations.

Plus, being rude goes against all of my natural urges. Once, after a rideshare driver shouted at me at the end of my journey for reasons I still don't understand, I gave him the finger and reported him to the ridesharing app. But then, rather than being pleased that I'd prevented him from shouting at other women, I spent several days feeling guilty for overreacting. Maybe he'd had a hard day? Maybe he didn't realize that shouting at me was wrong? Having spent so much of my life assuming that my feelings were either wrong or secondary to the feelings of others, rewriting the rules felt uncomfortable as all hell.

I've encountered a whole lot of self-help books in my time, which generally propose that they can fix your life with a few simple and easy steps. I cannot do that. All I can do is give you the tools to be more positively rude.

A Brief History of Rude

Before we can break the cycle of being afraid to be rude, we need to understand where that fear comes from. For most of us, it starts in childhood.

I realize that putting the blame on childhood isn't exactly revolutionary. But it's true. Our parents spend hours and hours trying to drill into us that we have to ask to leave the table when we've finished our food, wait quietly to speak, put our hands up in class, bless people when they sneeze, and put our hands over our mouths when we yawn. Now, some of this, I'm on board with. When I worked as a nanny I was an absolute stickler for saying please and thank you. It might sound counterintuitive, but I firmly believe that you can be rude while still having lovely manners.

I draw a line between the kind of politeness that costs you nothing and helps others (saying please and thank you, saying good morning to a receptionist or a doorman) and the kind of politeness that *Rude* should help you rebalance—specifically the kind of politeness that makes you think that your own needs, wants, and opinions are less important than those of the people around you.

15

Much of what we are taught when we're kids is about self-sacrifice. Your friend wants to play with your toy? Hand it over. There's only one piece of candy left? Give it to your sister. And while the intention is to create selfless, self-sacrificing adults, what it often does is create adults who believe that their own wants and needs should come at the absolute bottom of the pile, leaving them unable to be pushy or demanding when they need to be.

Little girls, I'm afraid to say, usually have it even worse. Just look at this nineteenth-century poem, thought to have been written by Robert Southey, which most of us will have heard on the playground or in nursery school:

> *What are little boys made of?*
> *What are little boys made of?*
> *Slugs and snails*
> *And puppy-dogs' tails*
> *That's what little boys are made of*
> *What are little girls made of?*
> *What are little girls made of?*
> *Sugar and spice*
> *And all things nice.*
> *That's what little girls are made of.*

Gender-neutral parenting is becoming more fashionable these days, but if you were born more than ten years ago and your parents weren't super-advanced gender scholars, the chances are you had a gendered childhood. That doesn't mean that you were forbidden from wearing blue or told that you weren't allowed to like football. Gender stereotyping is more insidious than that.

Your parents probably didn't mean to treat you differently from your brothers or any other little boys in your social group. But they likely still did, thanks to inherited stereotypes that are so common they barely register: "boys will be boys;" boys mature more slowly than girls; boys are naturally aggressive; boys need an outlet for their energy.

A 2018 study by *First News* found that the majority of children between nine and fourteen felt that they were treated differently because of their gender. One ten-year-old even commented that she had been told at school that she needed to be more "ladylike."

Rudeness is the absolute opposite of being ladylike. In fact, *Rude* throws a full martini in the face of ladylike and then sleeps with its husband. Being ladylike is about being sweet, quiet, and unprovocative and allowing life to happen around you while you put out more finger sandwiches. Being rude is about grabbing the world by the balls and twisting until you get what you want.

One of the most frustrating lines that children are subjected to is "girls mature more quickly than boys." According to clinical psychologist Dr. Hamira Ruiz, this claim hasn't been scientifically proven. She says, "While it is true that neuroscientists are making new discoveries about how the brain rewires itself during/after puberty and there is some MRI evidence to suggest that the adolescent female brain prunes itself differently and at a faster pace compared to the male brain, it is still a very big leap of inference to link neuronal changes in the brain to gender-specific behaviors."

But, regardless of what the science says—or doesn't say—the idea that girls mature more quickly than boys has become a self-fulfilling prophecy. Girls are held to a higher standard and made responsible for their actions from an earlier age, which means that we start thinking about—and worrying about—being rude while our brains are at their most elastic.

"Boys will be boys" is another one of those catchall expressions that has become an ingrained attitude. When I worked as a nanny, I spent many hours sitting on the edge of a playground, and thanks to my dodgy iPhone battery, I often didn't have anything to do but watch the children play. If you ever find yourself in the same situation, observe how childcare providers treat boys and girls differently. Girls are told far more frequently to let other children have a turn on the swings/slide/whatever the most interesting bit of the playground is.

There is an enduring perception that boys have more energy and mature more slowly, therefore they need to be allowed to run around, climb on furniture, interrupt their parents' conversations, and generally be rude.

Is it any wonder, given that we're taught it from our early childhood, that by the time we reach adulthood we, as women, struggle to be assertive in the workplace? As little girls we are told over and over again to wait our turn, to share nicely, to say please and thank you, and not to interrupt. Then as adults we wait our turn for a promotion. We share nicely instead of grabbing the space we need. We say please when we want to speak in a meeting or around the dinner table, and we say thank you when we're permitted the space to speak. We don't interrupt to ask for pay raises and we don't complain if we don't get them. We stay quiet when men put their hands up our skirts on public transport because we don't want to make a fuss. We tell men in bars that we don't want to have a drink with them because we have boyfriends, rather than telling the truth: that we just don't want to.

The problem is that in adulthood, the ability to push yourself forward becomes the hallmark of success. But in trying to teach us not to be rude, our parents programmed us to be the architects of our own oppression. The lessons that we are taught as little girls are the exact lessons that oppress us when we grow up.

1 | **RUDE** to Your Friends

The famous thinker Albus Dumbledore (order of Merlin, first class) once said, "It takes a great deal of bravery to stand up to our enemies, but just as much to stand up to our friends." Only, of course, it was J. K. Rowling who wrote those words, and she had a bloody good point: being rude to people whom you'll never see again is one thing; being rude to people who have known you for your entire life, and who have come to expect a certain type of behavior from you, is much harder. But our friends are some of the people we spend most of our time with, and they're also the people most likely to ask things of us, so we should learn how to be rude to them.

The film *Mean Girls* came out when I was thirteen. If you haven't seen it, put this book down and go and watch it, because honestly, it's the greatest cinematic triumph of all time and still deserves a retrospective Oscar nomination for Best Picture. For those who saw it in 2004 and not since, a brief refresher: Cady Heron moves back to the US after having been homeschooled in Africa. She's never experienced Western teenagers before and quickly learns that Girl World is a complicated, self-governing society within itself. The astonishing thing about the film is that the observations it makes about female friendships were as true of my friends at an all-girls school in East Sussex as they were about teenagers at a fictional high school in Illinois. No matter where, girls learned the ability to say, "I love your skirt," to a person's face and then seconds later, "That is the ugliest effing skirt I've ever seen," behind her back.

The cruelty that we inflicted upon one another as teenagers was beyond shocking. I made up rumors about people in our year sucking their own nipples, masturbating with Parker fountain pens, and having affairs with their riding instructors, because my ability to tell a good story made me worth having around. I peer-pressured, bullied, gossiped about, bitched about, and hurt the young women around me, and in turn had all of those things done to me. All of it sneaky, all of it underhanded. And this behavior didn't necessarily stop after our teen years.

Romantically, we behave—or at least try to behave— completely differently as adults from how we did as teenagers. We don't call men and hang up over and over again, or make up and break up three times in the same day. We don't tell our friends every minute detail of our sexual progress toward penetration and we don't let our friends decide whether we have feelings for someone or not. I noticed somewhere around the time I left college that while my attitude toward men and sex had changed as I'd gotten older, much of my behavior toward my friends (mainly talking about them behind their backs and worrying that they all hated me) had not. The only real difference was that we were gossiping over wine in our own apartments rather than Diet Coke in our parents' houses.

Friendship is a complex, tricky area that many of us struggle to navigate, but if you (like me) have sleepwalked into your twenties or thirties, still handling your friendships in the same way that you did in your teens, then it might be time to have a think about what needs to change.

Gossip, Aggression, and Anger

It's a bit of a generalization that male friendships and female friendships are inherently different, but anecdotally it seems to be true. Men and boys are more inclined toward telling their friends if they are annoyed with them, and even occasionally, as kids, resorting to physical violence. Women and girls are much less likely to tell each other when they are annoyed—or to hit each other. But that doesn't mean that we skip the fight. We just fight in an underhanded, sneaky way, because it's essential to keep a pretty face on at all times.

There is a tendency with modern feminism to blame the patriarchy for anything and everything, which can seem a little lazy, but . . . it turns out that it's often true. The pressure for women to always seem nice and to be sweet-natured peacemakers is an impossible burden to bear. So, in order to try to live up to that expectation, we avoid conflict with our friends by talking about them behind their backs.

From what I've observed, a man can sometimes stand up to another male friend simply by saying, "Fuck off, man." If I told one of my friends to fuck off, the entire conversation would grind to a halt. When one of my girlfriends upsets me, either I say nothing or I complain about it to someone else. If I really wanted to say something, it would mean going out for a drink and having a calm, measured discussion about how we had upset each other. And while there's nothing wrong with that—using your words to try to explain things rather than saying "fuck off" or throwing a punch is the better way to do things—women get a raw deal when it comes to conflict.

We feel that we have to play nice, so we rarely experience the catharsis of really blowing up at a friend. And because we're not allowed to just have the fight, and sometimes are too angry to want to have a measured conversation over a drink, we end up holding all of our anger in or bitching about each other. Sadly, we all know that if someone will bitch with you, they'll bitch about you, which means that any friend you enjoy an enormous gossip with is probably doing the exact same thing when your back is turned.

All research—and personal experience—shows that it's normal for people to need somewhere to put their anger. I've noticed that when I've been angered by an experience—being pushed on public transport, someone making a sharp comment during a meeting—I have found myself unable to shake my frustration afterward. But at least those experiences are transient. Friendships, by their very nature, are ongoing, and when we're frustrated with one of our friends but don't have an outlet for said frustration, it festers. I will often find myself raging about a relatively minor incident from a week before because I didn't allow my frustration any outlet.

While I don't suggest that you attend social events looking for a fight, allowing your rage some oxygen is genuinely important. By saying, "Bailing on our plans with short notice is really frustrating," or "I love hearing about your career success, but I'd like to talk about my work too," you remove the anger from your internal pressure cooker, which means you can move on, and avoid getting home and sending a stream of messages to a mutual friend about how much you hate your shared friend.

Groups and Breakups

The idea that women have neat little circles of female friends, all of whom adore one another, is something of a fiction. If you do have a group of girlfriends who live close together, are all equally close to one another, spend time doing activities and talking about their lives, and never get sick of one another, then you are a) killing it and b) living in a TV show directed by Darren Star.

The far, far more common way adult friendships manifest themselves is as a hodgepodge of different people from different stages of your life, all of whom are familiar with one another but mostly via you. It's also extremely likely that there will be a few people in your extended social circle whom you don't especially like but whom you keep in your life because they're part of the group and it would be more work to get rid of them than it is to pretend to care when they talk about their boyfriend/cat/job/craft projects. It's fine not to love everyone in your social circle equally, but when you get to the stage where you are spending hours of your life humoring someone you don't really like, you've got to ask why.

We all know how to break up with a romantic partner. The framework is easy to follow—you're supposed to be honest and, if you were in a serious relationship, do it in person. You most likely expect to feel sad afterward. After a while of wallowing, crying, and listening to Taylor Swift, you take up kickboxing, get a haircut, and bam, you're a brand-new woman. A little facetious, perhaps, but there is a routine and a ritual to a romantic breakup; it's almost like a sacrament. But we don't have anything of the sort when it comes to friendship breakups. In fact, even having a friendship breakup is unusual.

When I was a teenager, a friend and I decided to break up. We went out to lunch at PizzaExpress (the height of sophistication), had an afternoon of shopping in town (aka sitting on a bench in the mall), and then agreed that that was it: when we went back to school after the holidays we would be broken up and would focus on other friendships. It was pretty cringeworthy and a bit dramatic, all very befitting of being a teenage girl, but the central thesis was actually pretty solid. Admittedly it was probably motivated by the fact that we went to an all-girls school and didn't know any boys but wanted to experience a breakup. But there was a good sentiment at the core of it. We had ceased to be good friends to each other, so we decided to bring the relationship to an end. When it comes to dumping a romantic partner, women are able to supersede the rudeness of rejecting a long-term partner because the framework is well established and because we have societal permission to do so.

There's no such framework for friendship breakups. It doesn't occur to us that we're allowed to say "thanks but no thanks" to the women in our lives, so we limp along, going out for drinks with people who undermine and belittle us, or spending weekends hosting people who live on the other side of the country and talk exclusively about themselves for the entire trip.

I've been dumped by a friend as an adult, and it was the most traumatic breakup that I've ever had. We had been extremely close for five or six years, but I had changed a great deal in that time. She was older, established, and settled in her life, whereas I had gone from student to receptionist to writer, and gone from single to engaged over the course of our friendship. Initially I chalked her rejection up to an inability to cope with my changing fortunes. Our friendship had originally been based on a dynamic in which she was the older, wiser, and dominant friend and I was the sillier, younger, and sweeter one who did whatever she wanted whenever she wanted. For a while it worked—I liked having someone who organized my social life for me, who could advise me on the best course of action and generally be a sort of demi–mother figure, but as I got older and more independent I started to feel suffocated and patronized.

Eventually we had a fight and she blocked me on all methods of communication, as was her right. At the time I was devastated, but now I admire her for doing it. Unlike me, who clings to every friend I have lest I one day find myself unable to fill a Saturday night with plans, she was bold (rude) enough to decide she no longer wanted anything to do with me. In the long run, by doing the rude thing, she saved us both a lot of strained lunches, passive-aggressive WhatsApps, and resentful dinner parties.

Introducing Rudeness to Your Friendships

If you've always been a bit rude, then getting ruder isn't so hard. But if, like so many of us, you've either put on a nice-girl face or actually are a nice girl, then it's difficult to change that overnight and even more difficult to find a new, better balance without veering too far to one side. If you go from picking up other people's dry cleaning to turning down your best friend's thirtieth-birthday dinner because you'd rather stay home and watch *Love Island* (because you're just not in the mood), then you've overcorrected.

The obvious option is to go softly-softly. Slowly introduce a little bit of straight talking and then, in about a decade, you'll be able to skip a girls' night on the other side of your town that's being held at a raw vegan restaurant. But the problem there is that it doesn't really fit with the whole power-of-rude philosophy, does it?

The best way to introduce rudeness into your friendships is to make it mutual. The truth is that your friends want to cancel on you just as often as you want to cancel on them. Your heart might sink at the idea of sitting outside a rammed pub in central London watching them down glasses of wine, but they might have the same reaction to your suggestion of a nine a.m. Sunday run and brunch. Bringing the power of rude into your friendship isn't about your being the arbiter of everything. It's about saying to the people you love, "I don't think that we should do things that make us stressed or unhappy anymore. I'm going to start by telling you when I don't want to do something, or when I'm too tired or broke. And I'd really like you to do the same thing."

The power of rude isn't just about getting you out of doing things that you don't want to do—you'll always have to do some things you don't really feel like doing—it's about getting you to make an informed choice about how much of that stuff you are willing to do. It's never going to be okay to become totally selfish and only ever spend time on what you feel like doing—you're going to be very fat, poor, and unemployed if that's the case—but you have to be honest with yourself and other people and make a sensible assessment of each and every situation. Going to visit your grandparents? Important. Going to an expensive group meal with people you don't really know? Not so important.

My younger sister has an expression: "That sounds really nice, I don't want to come." It's a flippant turn of phrase, but it works. When I have tickets to a stand-up show five minutes from my house, which means she has to travel two hours, she uses it. When I try to convince her that she will enjoy coming to my adult ballet class? Same thing. An activity that thrills you might well leave someone else cold, and there's no use in pretending otherwise.

Before I wrote *Rude*, my friendships were without a doubt the place where I most needed to take my own medicine. A close friend had taken to making her child the center of every conversation. She'd also bring her along to every dinner without warning, despite having a co-parent and being able to afford a babysitter. Evenings where I wanted to smoke a cigarette, drink a large glass of wine, and swear at will became evenings of sitting in her living room and admiring how clever her small child was for picking up wooden blocks. So, I told her, face-to-face—not over WhatsApp like I wanted to—that I wanted to spend some adult-only time with her.

Initially it didn't go down well. She cried. Then she told me something along the lines of: "I don't think you're interested in my daughter, who is the focal point of my life. Becoming a mom has been incredibly hard and whether you are interested or not, you have an obligation as my friend to listen to me talk about things that are significant to me. I'm sorry that I'm not the friend you had before I had kids, but I'm not the same person anymore." She had a point.

Eventually, after a glass of wine, we came to a compromise: we would split our time together between my coming over, seeing both my friend and her child, and going out together like we used to. Since then, our friendship has been notably closer and more robust, and the way that we speak to each other has become more genuine. Initially, she felt that my rudeness was born of a lack of care, but in reality, the only reason I said something was because I value her so much. Because we both started being honest (rude), we both got what we needed, rather than spending the next decade quietly resenting each other.

Bringing the power of rude into your friendship will, almost certainly, create work. You'll need to explain and explore what it is that you want to change. But, if you're willing to put in the work, you might just see that, as funny as it sounds, being rude to your friends really can be an act of love.

Boundaries

In 2019, an academic named Melissa A. Fabello became briefly Internet famous after she suggested ways to send a sort of out-of-office message if friends got in touch looking for emotional support at a time when you weren't in a position to give it. She tweeted: "I am the kind of person who people reach out to when they're in pain. Because I'm good at emotional processing AND logical problem-solving, I tend to be a go-to for my friends who need to externally process their experiences. Too often, friends unload on me without warning—which not only interrupts whatever I'm working on or going through, but also throws me into a stressful state of crisis mode that is hard to come down from. Unless it is TRULY an emergency, that's unfair."

Initially I found myself irritated by Fabello's comments, but I am increasingly trying to examine my own motivation for my annoyance, and when I audited my frustration, I found that it stemmed from a rejection of her highly therapized way of speaking and my ingrained rejection of anyone who wants to put themselves first.

In reality, I understand Fabello's predicament: I'm also someone whom people come to if they need to talk; I'm a decent listener, I'm generally interested in other people's problems, and I will always have wine in the house. Perhaps, I realized as I read more about Fabello's theory, my anger at her way of handling needy friends was due to the fact that I had always assumed it was compulsory to drop everything and listen to someone else's issues on demand.

Fabello then suggested a template for how to respond to someone who has asked for your support at an inconvenient time. The template reads: "Hey! I'm so glad you reached out. I'm actually at capacity dealing with someone else who's in crisis/dealing with some personal stuff right now and I don't think I can hold appropriate space for you. Could we connect at [later date or time] instead/Do you have someone else who you can reach out to?" Again, on the first read I bristled, deciding that this was the absolute zenith of modern selfishness—and that she sounded like the kind of automated service you have to speak with if your Wi-Fi goes down. Given the barrage of replies, it was clear that Fabello had stumbled on something real—that it's true that we should put the needs of others before our own sometimes, but also that it is perfectly valid to tell someone you don't have room to hear about their horrible boyfriend for the fifteenth time.

While it might seem cruel and cold to tell someone that you're not in the mood to listen, it is okay to need space and to not have the bandwidth to help someone out any time day or night. Emergencies are emergencies and therefore an entirely separate thing. But, in terms of your average low-level request for support, boundaries are legitimate. If you set the expectation for the people you love that support will only be given when it can be given freely and without resentment, they might actually end up feeling more able to turn to you, rather than feeling abandoned.

Is it rude to tell your friend that you don't have the emotional energy to spend on them? Probably a bit, yes. Is it the right kind of rude? Probably also yes, depending on your reciprocal expectations. If you send a friendship out-of-office, you need to be entirely prepared to get one back.

Parents vs. Nonparents

One of the biggest gaps that exists between my friends is that between parents and nonparents. And this is true of society at large. There's a wage gap between women who do and do not have children, various social settings are either devoted to serving kids or barring them entirely, and if you debate any topic long enough, someone will put on a saintly voice and say, "As a parent . . . ," as if having a child validates their opinion above those of people who have committed to contraception.

One of the biggest hurdles any of us faces in long-term friendships is that, at some point, one of you will probably decide to move the goalposts by procreating. Suddenly, when you become a parent, all bets are off. Having a baby lobs a rock into the millpond of your friendship, and the ripples extend far beyond you and your partner. Don't get me wrong, becoming a parent is a miracle; however, it's also something that you choose for yourself but impose on everyone else in your life. I don't have children, but lots of my friends do, and I've seen firsthand how it unavoidably changes your relationships with them. However hard you try, there is a line between people with young children and people without them, and it's a line that makes the power of rude very complicated.

Let's take a classic (and real) dilemma: A woman who recently had a baby is due to go to a friend's birthday dinner in a few weeks' time. Her baby, who is exclusively breastfed and therefore cannot be left for the duration of the dinner, is three months old. She wants to bring the baby to the dinner—it will probably sleep through most of it—but her friend, who does not have children and is planning a big boozy night, does not want the baby to come because it will "change the dynamic," and if she says yes to one baby, other people might want to bring their kids as well.

It's a perfect example because no one is right and no one is wrong. The birthday girl doesn't want to be sitting in the middle of a new-moms' support group wearing a sparkly dress that someone's darling little angel eventually vomits on, but the friend doesn't want to become a social pariah because her baby—who probably, being asleep, would not distract from the party—cannot be left at home.

RUDE

If I were advising the birthday girl to be rude, I would tell her to pull rank: it's her birthday, so she makes the rules, and she wants a child-free evening, therefore she is entitled to have that. Were I advising the new mom, I would tell her that she has every right to ask her friends to make reasonable adjustments to include her and to let them know that if they're not willing to have the baby at the party, then sadly she won't be able to come. At the end of the day, all you can really do is try to be both rude and kind. Being rude does not mean suspending your humanity or your sense of decency.

In real life, the situation was (somewhat) solved by the mom attending just the early part of the dinner while her partner looked after the baby nearby. The birthday girl and the friend group made a huge fuss over the new mom while she was there, and everyone came away from it feeling they had at least tried.

Unfortunately, in my experience as a person who doesn't have children, the burden tends to fall mostly on us. I've spent a lot of time at birthday parties or soft-play centers playing hide-and-seek, waiting for a friend to ask a question about me, which never comes. It is hard, and it would be disingenuous to pretend otherwise; however, it's also enormously worthwhile. And, let's face it, if people stopped having babies, then the human race would come to a swift end. But it seems that much of the time the options are either to be honest or to be supportive, and there is no reason why you can't be both. Spend a Saturday morning in an aquarium with a screaming hangover and other people's kids, but be honest that you are there because you love your friend, not because you love child-centric weekend activities.

And share the fact that you're delighted to do it today, but you'd really like a martini in a dark bar, just the two of you, at some point in the near future.

When you allow yourself to be a little bit rude, which in this situation would have meant popping a note under the door saying either "I realize that it's your birthday but at the moment it's me plus baby or no me" or "I'm sorry that you can't come if you can't bring your baby, but it's an adult environment and I'd love to see you and your child another time," you take the heat out.

Again, it's about being the "right" kind of rude. Picking your moment. Phrasing it nicely. Sticking to your guns but not acting as if anyone is wrong or at fault. As is so often (annoyingly) the case when you're trying to navigate a friendship where one of you has had children, no one is right or wrong in this situation; talk to someone else and be as rage-filled as you want.

THE RIGHT KIND OF
Rude to Your Friends

▶ Your friends are some of the hardest people to be rude to, especially if you've known them for a long time and set the expectation that you will behave in a certain way. However, good friends will be understanding (if a little surprised) when you announce a regime change.

▶ It's normal for friendships to ebb and flow. It is not your responsibility to keep every single one of your friendships in perfect harmony at all times.

▶ Friendships should involve give-and-take. If you come away from every meeting feeling drained, having only talked about the other person, then that friendship is not working for you.

▶ When your friends have children, it will change their lives. You are not obligated to completely change yours, unless you want to.

▶ A little bit of bitching and gossiping is normal—women have been socialized to talk *about* each other rather than *to* each other. That said, if you are constantly expressing the same frustrations about the same person, that's a compass for your true feelings about them and you should follow it.

▶ Sometimes friendships need breakups, just like romantic relationships do.

▶ Friendship groups where everyone gets along brilliantly and you're all equally close to one another are fiction. Liberate yourself from that aspiration and you'll feel a whole lot freer.

▶ You are not an unpaid therapist and if someone is using you as such, you have the right to set boundaries.

▶ That said, you should expect people to mirror the boundaries you set for them. Being rude doesn't mean being unreasonable, and you can't do the three a.m. "Why doesn't he love me?" call if you've told your girlfriends that you will have friendship office hours between eleven and one on Tuesdays and Thursdays.

PRINCESS MARGARET

◄ ►

Born in 1930, Princess Margaret was the younger sister of Queen Elizabeth II. While being polite is sort of Queen Elizabeth's job description, Margaret was bound by no such rules. She was, without a doubt, a gloriously rude woman.

Margaret had a talent for leaning into her privilege. A diary of her daily routine written by her biographer claimed that she started the morning at nine a.m. with breakfast in bed, followed by two hours in bed listening to the radio, reading the newspapers ("which she invariably left scattered over the floor"), and chain-smoking. The job of a royal is mostly to cut ribbons, shake hands, and pretend that you're interested in whoever you're talking to. It's the very antithesis of being rude. And yet Margaret was uniquely skilled at something that so many of us struggle with: saying no.

The princess was once at a party in Chelsea when George Harrison, who had recently been arrested, charged, and released on bail for drug possession, came up to her and told her that he was in trouble. He claimed that the police had "planted a big block of hash in [his] bedroom closet." Harrison asked Margaret whether she might be able to get the charges dropped, which she almost certainly could have done. Rather than feeling the need to offer to try, she simply said, "I don't really think so. It could become a little sticky."

Since time immemorial, princesses have been used in stories to guide little girls into behaving a certain way. Cinderella, the most famous princess of all, is rewarded with a pretty dress, some new shoes, and a rich husband because she suffers through an abusive childhood without complaint. Not exactly a message fit for the modern age. Princess Margaret could not have been further from the simpering sweetness of Cinderella.

In his Princess Margaret biography, *Ma'am Darling*, Craig Brown writes that Derek Jacobi once found himself slapped on the wrist during lunch with Princess Margaret: "There were eight of us and I sat next to her. She smoked continuously, not even putting out her cigarette when the soup arrived, but instead leaning it up against the ashtray. We got on terribly well, very chummy, talking about her mum and her sister, and she really made me feel like I was a friend, until she got a cigarette out and I picked up a lighter and she snatched it out of my hand and gave it to another dancer named David Wall. 'You don't light my cigarette, dear. Oh no, you're not that close.'"

Harsh? Absolutely. But again, a skill. How many of us have

allowed people to be uncomfortably overfamiliar with us and said nothing, for fear of seeming stuck-up? Margaret had no such qualms. Her friend Anne Glenconner writes in her autobiography, *Lady in Waiting*, that Margaret "hated" whenever anyone tried to light her cigarette. When she didn't like something, rather than putting up with it, she made a fuss. Given the number of women I know who are terrified of making a fuss, perhaps it is Princess Margaret we need as a role model, not Cinderella.

2 | RUDE
to Your
Family

As children, we often assume that other people's families are better than our own. Your friends from school invariably had a better type of cereal than you did or were allowed to get their ears pierced much younger than you were. And then, sometime in your twenties, you realize that everyone's family is messed up, but that there is a kind of Fibonacci sequence of fucked-upness, which enables everyone to have their own special brand of mad.

All families have a different attitude toward in-family rudeness. If you come from a very traditional family, it is likely that you were raised to always show extreme deference to your parents. I wasn't raised that way. In fact, the area of my life where I am most at ease with rudeness is with my family. I call my parents by their first names, drink with them, smoke in front of them, and talk openly and honestly about my feelings, and as such we're an incredibly close-knit family. My parents and siblings (and my husband) are my favorite people to spend time with.

I attribute our closeness now to our rudeness to one another when my siblings and I were growing up. When I was a teenager and my friends' parents were putting down rules left, right, and center, my parents honestly didn't give a fuck. They had a vibrant social life, loads of friends, and no interest in spending time with their children if it was under duress. The only sacrosanct part of the week was Sunday lunch. Much like lots of Jewish families have Friday night dinner, we had Sunday lunch. A period of the week where we all sat around the table and talked about everything. There's an old saying that you should avoid discussing sex, religion, and politics at the table. My family sees that more as a to-do list than a list of topics to be avoided. Sunday lunch topics over the years have included anal bleaching, sex tapes, and how the Kardashian family works (my father can just about name the main siblings, but the children evade him).

As far as I'm concerned, my parents were the perfect rude parents. They had busy lives and they didn't sacrifice their desires for our every whim. They wanted us to be busy enjoying our friends and exploring the world, and they created a safe and warm place with wine and cake to come back to if and when we needed to. Failure was encouraged, debate was obligatory, and anyone who waited for an invitation to speak would find that she was silent for a long time.

My husband visited my family for the first time after we'd only been dating for a few months. He arrived with a bottle of wine and lots of nice manners, but by the end of that first dinner, he was shell-shocked. We'd been screaming at one another across the table, debating something (probably Brexit or *Love Island*), and everyone was drinking, swearing, and interrupting one another—just about managing not to throw food, but only just. My sweet husband from a well-mannered, nicely behaved family had arrived expecting a placid evening of polite conversation and had accidentally stumbled into the rudeness epicenter of the UK.

Of course, not all of us were raised in a family that tolerated rudeness, and even for those of us who were, it is still often hard to introduce new forms of positive rudeness into your family dynamic. Making any kind of change within the family unit is difficult, especially when it comes to how we interact with our parents. Very often, our parents put us into boxes when we're children. It doesn't matter if you've got a modeling contract and your sister has a Nobel Prize—if when you were children your parents assigned you the "clever" label and her the "pretty" one, then those labels will stick.

In my experience, any active or conscious choice to change yourself creates strife within a family unit. It's born of a good thing—hopefully, your family loves you and therefore doesn't feel that you need to change. Change is scary and often looks like a rejection of the past.

If you have the kind of parents who think that deference to elders is of paramount importance and continue to see you as a child into adulthood, I'll be honest with you: it's worth assessing whether you are up for the fight. If you want to have a genuine and honest relationship with your parents, then yes, you do need to tell them that you are bisexual, that you're vegan, that you're living with your boyfriend out of wedlock, or that you're quitting your job to start your own cushion-making business. But it's also entirely reasonable to evaluate what you will get out of positive rudeness toward your family and if the trade-offs are worth it.

You are not a failure if the power of rude needs to stop at your parents' front door. Lots of people play a role when they are back home with their parents. Some parents will never understand their children's life choices, and trying to force them to understand you and your lifestyle may ultimately be a losing battle that will only serve to make you unhappy. News management is not a failure. Presenting your parents with what they want to see and then going home to live your authentic life is not wrong. Perhaps that's a kind of positive rudeness unto itself.

Regression

One of my habits that I most dislike is that when I go home to my family's house, especially at Christmas, I become a teenager again. Every single December I resolve that I will not let it happen, and yet by Christmas Eve I am physically fighting with my sister for the remote control and throwing a fit because I don't think that my brother is pulling his weight with washing dishes. Experts have suggested that we owe this regression to the fact that when we physically put ourselves back in time, we therefore follow suit emotionally. There's no doubt that that is true. But I think it's also about lingering feelings and resentments that you may never have expressed.

Your parents will have hurt you at some point. If, as an adult, you've got a decent relationship with your parents, then you probably don't want to bring these past hurts up. Why drag it all up again? Why look for an argument? Why be rude? But here's the thing: if you don't risk upsetting your parents and lancing those boils, they just get bigger, angrier, and more painful. When you go home and steep yourself in the memories of childhood or adolescent hurt but don't allow yourself any outlet for your pain, you force yourself back into that impotent childlike state where your emotions were written off as "being hormonal" and you didn't get much of a vote because you were "one of the kids." Suddenly you're back in your bedroom, slamming doors and playing loud music because they're the only ways that you can have control over your environment.

When I was a teenager, my parents were very concerned about my weight, which seems odd because I wasn't an especially heavy child. Not skinny, but just sort of normal. But normal wasn't okay to them, so they tried all sorts of things: getting me a personal trainer, forcing me to do obligatory exercise before I was allowed to watch TV, offering me a whole new wardrobe if I lost weight.

Unsurprisingly this only served to make me completely,

absolutely, utterly obsessed with my weight. It is, without question, the thing that I have expended the most energy thinking about by this point in my life. I am angry about that, and I do, to an extent, blame my parents. Thanks to their interest, bordering on obsession, with my weight, I experimented with bulimia and I've been either on a diet or bingeing because I've fallen off a diet since I was thirteen.

I never talk to them about any of this, even though it still nags at me. But I don't want to kick that wasp nest. I don't want to throw all the glorious things about my idyllic childhood back at them because they looked ashen faced when I wanted to eat an ice-cream bar. But there is a price to pay for my refusal to be "rude" to them about their relationship with my weight. When I am around them, food, weight, body image—it's all a tinderbox. I definitely can't enjoy pigging out on anything and everything I want to eat on festive family occasions (unless I've been dieting and look/feel thinner than usual). I plan outfits for family occasions based on how small they make me look. I think about my body—something I have made a fragile peace with in my own home—constantly when I am back in my childhood bedroom.

The chances are that you also have your own areas of sensitivity toward your family. Maybe it's not your weight. It might be your sexuality, your career, your dating history—the possibilities are endless—but there is probably something that feels too painful to try to course-correct with your parents. There are people who refuse to accept this, who speak candidly to their families about the scar tissue that they created, and probably come out of the whole experience stronger and better for it. But if you're like me and there are some no-go areas cordoned off with barbed wire, that's okay too. You can introduce smaller elements of being rude while also leaving some things in the past.

I mentioned earlier in this chapter that it's hard to get your long-term friends and family members to accept that you can change. Sometimes it is about showing rather than telling them. Eat a second helping of pasta under the eye of a disapproving auntie who thinks you should be a size 4 to get a man. Tell a prying cousin that you're not open to answering questions about your dating life. You are an adult now, and while going home might make you feel like a teenager again, you are not.

Partners

A few months after I started going out with my husband, I was in the bath at his house and I accidentally flooded the floor. I was mortified. I apologized fifteen, twenty times, acting like I'd killed his best unicorn. Six months later I accidentally shrank his sweater in the washing machine—a sweater that I happened to hate. I laughed so hard at the teeny-tiny sweater and his outrage at its loss that I thought I might rupture something. My point here is that somewhere between the bath and the sweater, I stopped being polite to him.

We talk a lot about the honeymoon period in a relationship and how hard it is when that time of never-ending bliss comes to an end. Yes, it is a bummer when the day comes that the very idea of seeing your boyfriend naked ceases to send you into a tailspin. At this point, you'll likely have stopped getting out of bed to brush your teeth before pretending to have just woken up minty fresh. Things are changing. But this is also the time when you, hopefully, stop being afraid of being rude to your partner.

You cannot build a life with a person whom you're afraid to be rude to. The key is to make it the kind of rudeness that makes you closer. When our honeymoon period drew to a close, I held an amnesty with my husband (boyfriend at the time), a chance to tell all the uncomfortable truths that we needed to tell in order to move forward. "I didn't actually do an economics advanced-placement test," I started, citing a lie I'd told during a debate in our early days. "I don't like falling asleep cuddling," I told him, because after six months of a cricked neck and twisted spine it was time to put sleep quality above cuteness. "And I think that pub in Waterloo that you love is one of the worst places I've ever been drinking in my life."

I said it nicely, and I said lots of things that I loved about him, too. Then I asked him to do the same. He was tentative, sensing that this might be some kind of a trap, but eventually he told me that he thought I made a shit cup of tea (true), that he didn't want to listen to Taylor Swift every single day (we're still fighting on that one), and that sometimes when I make jokes at his expense it hurts his feelings.

Rudeness—that is to say, candidness—is the bedrock that we built our marriage on. And while our marriage is a long, long way from perfect, rudeness has made it infinitely better.

These days we have a marriage Moment of Truth every couple of months. We wait until we're in a really good mood with each other and feeling fully loved up, then we go to dinner, drink a bottle of wine, and talk about what's working, what's not working, what we want to change, and what we want to do more of. My husband hasn't always found this easy—he's one of life's repressors—but he would tell you (or at least he tells me) that it's a central part of what makes us work as a couple.

In-laws

The only parents more difficult to deal with than your own are your in-laws. I'm fortunate because my husband's parents are enormously tolerant of me, despite the fact that I regularly go on television to talk about my sex life. But when I first met them, I was terrified. I've never been keener to repress my entire personality than I was on my initial visit to stay with them. I was so busy trying be perfect that I stopped concentrating on anything other than being polite, which was how I ended up leaving a pair of my underwear in my husband's childhood bed and eschewing every single one of my political and social opinions, lest I give offense. Often, our fear of being rude translates to an obsession with getting it "right," sometimes to the point where we end up getting it completely wrong.

While I'm lucky with my in-laws, that's not always the case. And when you're saddled with the combination of bad in-laws and a desire not to offend said in-laws, you get a powder keg. Darhla is twenty-eight. She recently had a six-month-long relationship with a man named Oliver. A few months in, he took her back to his family home, a sizable demi-mansion in the

Home Counties. "It was all fine," she told me, "until his mom asked me what form of contraception I was using. She gave me this look when she asked, like refusing to answer would be unacceptable, and when I laughed it off, she seemed to think I had admitted that I was trying to baby-trap her son.

"Then after dinner, while we were having coffee and liqueurs, she brought out a bag of cocaine and offered everyone a line. I ended up doing one to be polite, as if it were a second helping of lasagna."

Admittedly Darhla's experience is pretty extreme; most of our mothers-in-law don't casually offer out Class A drugs as a chaser to a lovely tiramisu. But testing the boundaries and dick-swinging contests are very common. In-laws who want to make your life difficult realize that you're terrified of offending them. Of all the times that you're least likely to want to enjoy the power of rude, it's during a visit to your in-laws, but, however counterintuitive it might sound, that's why it's so important to pull out the rude straightaway.

Rose, twenty-eight, has been going out with her boyfriend, Matt, for seven years. "We go on holiday with his parents every year," she tells me, "because he's an only child and they're a very close-knit family. I knew that when I got involved. He's never going to stop going on the holiday with them, so either he goes on his own or I come along. In theory, it would be fine, but his father seems to get a real kick out of winding me up. I work in wine, so whenever we're drinking a bottle, he'll hide the label and get me to guess what grape it is. If I'm wrong, he absolutely loves it.

"Plus, he talks to me like I'm a little Victorian orphan, saying things like, 'I know it's a big villa that we're renting, don't worry, it wasn't that expensive, you don't need to chip in,' even though I've offered to and they won't let me. My boyfriend chooses not to see it; he says it's his dad being playful, so I nod and smile and think about the super-budget old-people's home I'm going to put him in one day."

Rose is in a difficult situation. She's not going to end her relationship, which is the better part of a decade old, in order to avoid her boyfriend's dad, and she's not confident enough to push back when he talks down to her. Her most practical (rude) option would be to either respond to the actual comments—"You're so kind to pay for the villa, though Matt and I did make it clear that we were very happy to contribute"—or, if the problem is too large at this point, be totally candid and say to Matt, "The way that your father speaks to me makes me feel patronized and uncomfortable, so I'll be sitting family holidays out for a while. You're more than welcome to go on these trips without me, of course."

We as humans like and respect strong people. Weakness is not an attractive quality. So, when you resist your boyfriend's mom as she offers you another super-strength gin and tonic, you're not being rude (in the bad sense), you're demonstrating that you're your own woman. Your in-laws will not like you more if you waver in your vegetarianism because they forgot and cooked sausages.

There is a popular phrase: "You don't have an in-law problem, you have a husband problem." If your other half is willing to watch his parents be rude to you, he's the real issue there, not them. And I agree—the most important thing about rude in-laws is to make sure that you and your partner are on the same page. If you go back to his childhood bedroom after supper and he starts telling you off for debating with his mother or for saying no to his father's suggestion of another helping of mashed potatoes, then run. Don't get involved with someone who automatically sides with his parents over you—that way lies ruin.

Extended Family

Every year, as the leaves turn golden and the air turns cold, people all over the world gird their loins as they prepare to return home and survive a barrage of offensive, inappropriate, and frustrating questions from their family. The Thanksgiving or Christmas dinner table is one of the only places in the world where you can watch a genderqueer vegan sit next to a Mike Pence–loving boomer. There should be something nice about the idea of everyone's reaching across political lines to celebrate the holidays together, but, in reality, it just seems to bring out the worst in all of us.

Embracing the power of rude does not mean getting into a fight every single time someone tries to start one. In fact, it is the opposite. Being positively rude is about not giving people what they want—unless you feel you have to give in. When a member of your extended family tries to start a "debate" about immigration or feminism, or pretty much anything, the most positively rude thing you could do is refuse to rise to the occasion, to smile nicely and say, "I'm not sure this is for the table, Uncle Simon. More peas?"

Trying to "educate" the people around you about why their trash opinions are trash is very noble, but you are never going to change someone's mind if they aren't open to listening to you. If you know that there's no way your potential sparring partner will approach the conversation with an open mind, rising to the occasion will just entail lots of emotional labor on your part, and will likely lead to other members of the family saying something infuriating like "Oh, you wind each other up!" or "You're each as bad as the other!" If anyone at this dinner is actually open to hearing what you have to say, then knock yourself out and throw facts about immigration or maternity rights their way, but at least make an honest assessment beforehand as to whether your emotional labor is worth it.

Motherhood

I think of my mother as, overall, an amazing parent. She made mistakes, obviously, and there were times when we screamed at each other, and weeks when I considered her to be my mortal enemy, but now, as I've reached my late twenties, my mom is one of my closest friends.

My mother, however, feels like she failed me during childhood. She carries guilt about the fact that she worked when we were children, that she had childcare, and that she wasn't willing to suspend her every wish the moment that her kids arrived in the world. The things that I most admire about her—her career, her social life, the fullness of the life that she lived around having children—are the things that she feels worst about. While I view her as the archetypal positively rude parent, I'm quite sure she would tell you that she felt like she was messing up pretty much the entire time.

I'm not a parent, and so it would be wrong for me to attempt to give any parenting advice, but what I have observed as someone with parents is that, more than most other things in life, parenting seems to have the capacity to make you feel like you're messing everything up—even if you're not. You might know on paper that leaving your child with a babysitter or at day care is right, but the baby's cries make it feel wrong. You might be totally convinced that spending time on your own or with your friends is an essential part of retaining your sanity, but again, when you're out in a pub sneaking off to the bathroom to look at pictures of your baby on your phone, it feels as if you're going against the grain of motherhood.

When you become a mother, you suddenly have to advocate both for yourself and for your child. The world seems to temporarily become your enemy, a place full of physical and emotional barriers. Maybe it's the flights of stairs with no elevators for your stroller, or the fact that strangers will happily comment on your choice to bottle- or breastfeed or on your baby's napping schedule. And your options at this point are to drown in your own guilt or to embrace the power of rude. I was happily surprised to see, though, that many of the mothers I surveyed while writing this book said that they actually felt braver and more confident after they had children—though that confidence was more often reflected when they were advocating for their children rather than for themselves.

Given that our phobia of being rude was most likely given to us by our parents ("They fuck you up . . . ," and all that), it follows that we have a choice as to whether or not to pass that phobia on to our own kids.

The most common theme I have heard from people who currently have young children is that they will no longer make their children hug or kiss family members and friends if they don't want to. "I was always forced to kiss all of my parents' friends and family goodbye when we left a party," says Sophie, who now has two daughters.

"To this day, I'll try to leave a party without saying goodbye to everyone, on the basis that I hate it. When my daughter was younger, I read an article about how you shouldn't make your kids kiss or hug anyone they don't want to, so that you teach them to have autonomy over their bodies. It's an easy way to teach them about consent from a really early age. When I read it something just clicked, but I also felt really angry—like I'd been let down by my own childhood. My parents prioritized the feelings of other adults above mine. They taught me, admittedly without meaning to, that it was rude to withhold physical affection from people who made me uncomfortable, a lesson that I continued to believe for much of my life."

Many women I interviewed expressed that they had an easier time being rude on behalf of their children than on behalf of themselves. This makes sense: it's more viable to suspend the rules ingrained in you in order to protect your child rather than to take care of yourself.

But in some cases, motherhood empowered women to be more positively rude, period. Gabrielle is thirty-five and she has one daughter. She told me a story that exemplified the change that motherhood can inspire: "I was in a café with my daughter when she was a few months old. She'd barely slept the night before but was finally chilling out in the pram, sleepy and not making a fuss. I was playing on my phone, looking at everyone else's weekends and feeling jealous of everyone who'd gone out to the pub and hadn't needed to put nipple towels in their bra to soak up breast milk. A woman at the next table remarked to her husband that it's 'so sad how you only ever see mothers on their phones these days' and I lost my mind.

"I am not a confrontational person; I hate a fight. But I couldn't let it go. I interrupted and told her that I'd been alone with the baby for four days because my husband was traveling and that this was the first moment I'd had to myself, that it was none of her business, and to leave me alone. She was horrified, and then apologetic. Then they left. And I felt triumphant because I'd always been the person who came up with the perfect retort four hours later or bit my tongue because I didn't want to have an argument, but here I was shouting at this total stranger for mom-shaming me."

After hearing this, my main question for Gabrielle was how she felt afterward. Did she regret losing her temper and giving way to her anger? Apparently not. "I shouldn't have shouted," she says. "I should have said it calmly, but I was glad I said something, and honestly if the options were lose my temper or say nothing, I'm glad I lost my temper. She needed to know that you can't try to make people feel bad about their parenting for fun."

While Sophie might have been on the slightly more aggressive side of what this book endorses, it's certainly true that the feeling of wishing you had said something is corrosive. Sometimes it is okay to respond—and to respond with force.

Of course, even if we raise our kids to be positively rude, they still might not grow up to be positively rude adults. However much my parents embodied positive rudeness when I was growing up, I still once had a threesome because I didn't want to be impolite. So even great rude parents can turn out children who struggle to say the word "no." But more on that story later!

THE RIGHT KIND OF
Rude to Your Family

- You do not owe your family a free pass to do or say whatever they please toward you just because you are related. Anyone who makes you feel bad about yourself or your life is fair game for the rude treatment.

- Some people are not close with their family. That is okay. You have not failed because you don't get along with your siblings or because your mom is not your best friend. Sometimes family are the people you choose.

- Other people's families are incredibly difficult to navigate—it's okay if you never really nail it with your in-laws.

- However, as long as you are acting reasonably, your partner should be on your side, or at least try to play an active role in smoothing any friction between you and his family. As the saying goes, you don't have an in-law problem, you have a partner problem.

- Starting your own family (or rather, continuing it—two people can of course be a family on their own) is a scary business, but it does give you a chance to assess which parts of your own childhood were not ideal and think about how you want to counter them.

▶ It's easy to take a very black-and-white attitude toward your childhood: either it was happy or it was unhappy. But, in reality, it was most likely a mixture of both. Needing to talk to your parents about the unhappy aspects of your childhood does not mean that you are ungrateful. Confronting the issues head-on, rather than letting them fester, will help you have a healthy adult relationship.

MEGHAN MARKLE, THE DUCHESS OF SUSSEX

◀ ▶

Meghan Markle was born in 1981 in Los Angeles, California. Then, thirty-something years later, she met a prince, she fell in love, and the entire world lost its fucking mind.

The Demanding Duchess, Birth Brat, Princess Pushy—the insulting nicknames came thick and fast, sometimes even from members of her own family. For the high crime of not wanting to erase her entire personality and set of values (she's a proud feminist), Meghan has been crucified in the press over and over again. If she sneezes, she's spreading germs to innocent people. If she uses a tissue, she doesn't care about the mass slaughter of trees. I'm exaggerating here, but only a little bit.

Meghan may be a kindred spirit to many of us in the sense

that she is not naturally rude. When she first started to take part in royal life, she did pretty much everything she could possibly have done to make the British public and the royal family like her. Remember when she went to a family function a few days after her wedding wearing the world's most horrific "nude" tights? Remember how she went on a daylong train journey with her husband's grandmother? And smiled at children day after day after day? Then, like me, and hopefully like you, she had had enough. She realized that smiling and waving and being sweet weren't going to get her what she wanted (and what she wanted was basically to marry the man she loves, help out in the family business, and get on with it). She embraced the power of rude.

It started small. Well, as small as guest-editing the September issue of British *Vogue* can possibly be. Despite the fact that Prince Charles had guest-edited *Country Life* and the Duchess of Cambridge had guest-edited the Huffington Post, Meghan was lambasted for breaking the "no politics" rule, as she'd put women, including Greta Thunberg and Jane Fonda, on the cover.

Then the Sussexes started to make decisions based on what they wanted—breaking away and forming their own charity, not giving their son a royal title. Predictably, the press went mad over this. They were punished for decorating their house when the details of their refurb ended up online, sandwiched next to the words "taxpayers' money," as if the entire royal deal isn't taxpayers' money. The *Vogue* cover was smacked down with public critique of their use of a private jet. The couple's choice not to make the birth of their son a fully public event resulted in opinion pieces about how they "owe" the public photos of their child, along with some catty side-eye about Meghan's "post-birth body."

Many women would have curled back into their shell, chastised by a media attempt to shut them up, and abandoned the power of rude. But not Meghan. Instead, she and Harry took the unprecedented step of contacting a lawyer—their own lawyer, not the royal family's default firm—and announcing that Meghan was suing the *Mail on Sunday* for reproducing a letter she sent to her father, Thomas Markle, without her consent.

The lawsuit wasn't where the story ended, though. A few weeks later the couple embarked on a press tour of South Africa, accompanied by filmmaker Tom Bradby. During the course of the documentary, he asked Meghan about her experience of joining the royal family. Meghan answered candidly, prioritizing telling the truth above sparing anyone else's feelings in a way that had me punching the air. "Thank you for asking if I'm okay," she told the camera. "Not many people have."

Social media, the press, the entire bloody country went into overdrive: "ungrateful," "spoiled," "entitled." Commentators asked how a woman with so much money could possibly dare to say that she was having a hard time. And while it's true that the backdrop of South Africa, a country with its fair share of issues, perhaps didn't make for the perfect optics for a conversation about struggle, the point is, Meghan had broken the number one rule of being a royal: she'd spoken freely and openly about her feelings, not with a polished statement written by a group of professionals, but with her own voice. It was bold, brave, brilliant, and rude.

And Meghan is an icon of positive rudeness. She's probably one of the most polite people living in the UK right now. She literally spends her days shaking hands, smiling at children, and engaging in boring conversations with people she doesn't know. Her occupation is being charming. But she is still the right kind of rude. She has her own internal line, and if someone crosses said line, they will be made aware that it is not acceptable to do so. Meghan is a perfect example of the fact that being a rude woman doesn't mean being charmless or bad mannered. You can still be sweet, loving, generous, and polite—but all on your own terms.

NB: At the time of writing, Harry and Meghan have just handed in their notice to the royal family—the ultimate air-punching act of well-executed rudeness. Meghan has predictably been blamed, shamed, and called every name under the sun, which is what happens when women act as they see fit. But with a move to Canada, rumors of a Disney voice-over deal, and the family she loves around her, it looks like her rudeness was entirely worth it.

3 | RUDE
About
Dating

Full disclosure: it's been a little while since I was on the dating scene. I met my husband when I was twenty-two, got engaged at twenty-four, and got married at twenty-six. When I announced that I was getting hitched, various people asked me if I thought I was going to miss out on things by getting into a committed relationship so young, which seems like an odd thing to ask a newly engaged woman, but that's neither here nor there. The answer was a solid and reverberating no. I was not sad about it, because I didn't want to date. Dating, in my (admittedly limited) experience, is an absolute hellscape, and the five years that I'd spent having sex, relationships, and everything in between had been messy, painful, and complicated—and made worse by the fact that I, like many women, was blighted by an inability to offend.

When I used to go clubbing as a teenager, my friends and I would dance in a circle. Men would come up to us, grab our hips, and start dancing behind us, which pretty much just meant rubbing their crotches against our asses/backs, depending on how tall we were. Often that meant having a stranger's semi-erect penis gyrating against the small of your naked back (it was the early 2000s; low-waisted jeans were the thing). Rather than pulling away or even asking security to remove the penis-rubber, my friends and I would just rotate the circle until we reached a different portion of the dance floor in safety. We never made a fuss. Because, as you'll notice is rather a theme here, we didn't want to be rude. We assumed that because we were dressed up and dancing, these men had a right to attempt to fuck us, and that it was our responsibility to let them down gently.

Dating is now more commonly about apps than clubs, but the central point remains the same. Politeness is apparently the rent that women are obliged to pay for attempting to navigate the world of dating.

Rude to Be Kind

When I was in college, I dated a very sweet guy who had a well-paid job in the Middle East. He was a tax exile and was allowed to spend only ninety days a year in the UK, so to see each other we had to meet in various European cities. I was smitten and initially very into this arrangement. As a broke student, the whole thing was desperately exciting. It worked well at first: we spent a happy week traveling around Paris and the South of France, and I couldn't quite believe my luck. But a couple of months later I went back to school, got tangled up in my life as a student, and realized that international affairs weren't going to work for me anymore.

What I should have done was tell him straight that I'd had a brilliant time but that I'd decided we should stop seeing each other. But having spent my whole life avoiding offending people who had been mean to me, I had no idea how I was supposed to be honest with someone who had been nothing but kind. I was due to visit him in Italy, and as the date of my flight grew closer, I became more and more panicked. The day before the flight I came down with the flu and developed an abscess on my gum, meaning that I could hardly eat anything, but still I packed my bags, flew to Italy, and desperately tried to put on a brave face.

Upon arrival I practically passed out and spent the afternoon watching *Harry Potter* in the fancy hotel bed. I couldn't eat anything at the nice restaurants, could barely bring myself to finish a cocktail. I was horrible company and completely miserable. We would both have been happier if I had stayed at home in bed, but of course he was being so generous and kind, and I was so terrified of being ungrateful, that I'd ended up giving us both a miserable weekend.

We broke up on the Sunday morning after a calm and resigned conversation at breakfast. I took a bus back to the airport because I didn't want to inconvenience him by sticking around his hotel room, arrived six hours too early for my flight, and slept off the flu on an airport floor. If I'd had the confidence to say no to the trip, I'd have saved myself a lot of time and aggravation, but I'd also have saved him some as well. My desire not to be rude made me the absolute worst version of myself.

As with the above example, often we fear being rude because we don't want to hurt someone's feelings. But in those cases, our refusal to be positively rude is just as much about protecting ourselves from uncomfortable conversations. While attempting to avoid causing any hurt is noble and nice, it can end up being more hurtful to everyone involved. It's impossible to have a meaningful relationship with someone if you are afraid to hurt their feelings or to be rude to them.

If I told you that someone was "scared of being rude" you would probably automatically assume that this meant they were nice. But that's the thing: not being rude doesn't automatically make you nice. It made me conflict averse, which in turn made me a coward. Sometimes we let our desire to be liked or loved stop us from doing what is right.

That feeling—that you want to be loved—is even worse when you're dating. In the early days, there's a huge pressure to represent yourself as the best of the best. Generally speaking, that means that men and women dial up the values they are traditionally expected to exemplify: men act bold and brash and outgoing; women act sweet and kind and supportive, which (yes, you know what's coming) is the opposite of rude.

Tinder, Bumble, Hinge, and
God Knows What Comes Next

When I met my husband and hung up my dating hat, Tinder was still a new-ish phenomenon that came with a healthy side of stigma—as if being on Tinder meant you had stooped so low that you had to go trawling for Internet boyfriends on a sex website. Half a decade on, dating apps are pretty much the default, at least for people my age. In lots of ways they're a miracle. Apps make it easier to meet people who are outside of your social circle; they've reduced the popularity of dating in the workplace, which often makes life very awkward; and they allow people with specific or niche interests to connect with one another. But there's also no denying that operating from behind a screen has changed things. Dating apps have blurred the boundaries of acceptable human behavior.

Men in real life very rarely expose themselves to women, yet unsolicited dick pics are a way of life for the modern dater. Similarly, online dating has given rise to a whole host of nasty behaviors with catchy names, including but not limited to: catfishing, ghosting, zombieing, submarining, bread-crumbing, and benching. All of which stem from a fear of being the good kind of rude, which means behaving in the bad kind of rude way.

An easy example: I once went on a date with a man who had chronic asthma, thought that arts funding should be cut, and didn't like swearing. At the time, I was a committed smoker and aspiring playwright whose favorite word was "fuck." After we clawed our way through a ninety-minute drink, we went in opposite directions in both a literal and metaphorical sense. There was no question that we would ever see each other again, and yet, to his credit, he sent me a text saying that he didn't think the chemistry was there but that he enjoyed the bar I had chosen. Job done. As it happens, I was not on the edge of my seat hoping that he would message me, but, if I had been, I'd have read the message, been briefly deflated, and then moved on with my life.

On the flip side, on another occasion I went for a drink with a man I'd met through a temping job. I was drowning in a massive crush on him. Everything about him did it for me. We went for a drink and I hung on his every word, and then we entered into a protracted back-and-forth messaging situation where he would suggest meeting up and then cancel, again and again and again. Eventually he demi-ghosted me. During this period, whenever I met someone who might have been a sensible romantic prospect, I wrote them off instantly because as soon as Rupert changed his mind and realized I was the perfect woman, we were going to fall in love and get married.

I have no doubt that Rupert would tell you that he was "letting me down gently," but what he was actually doing was being the wrong kind of rude. Good rude is direct, fair, and tactful. Bad rude is self-serving and selfish. And while I didn't meet Rupert on an app, all my research (through friends and the *Rude* survey) shows that this sort of rudeness has increased exponentially in the dating app years.

Sorry, I Have a Boyfriend

I'm not sure when as a woman you learn to say, "Sorry, I have a boyfriend," to men in clubs and bars, but it's early on. I remember standing at the bar at a club in West London, freshly eighteen and waiting to buy one of my first legal drinks. An older guy in a suit started chatting me up, and when I went to return to my friends, he tried to come with me. It didn't occur to me to tell him that I wasn't interested or that I wanted to spend the evening with my friends. I, like so many women, reached for the automatic get-out-of-jail-free card: "I have a boyfriend." The problem there is that you're effectively using belonging to someone else as a justification for being left alone, when in reality you don't owe any explanation at all.

The I-have-a-boyfriend line is designed to allow a man to think that were you not in a committed relationship with someone else, you would be available for him to pursue. It is a way to reject a man without his realizing that he has been rejected, therefore insulating him from any negative emotions. You could argue that it's a victimless crime—you get left alone and he's allowed to enjoy his evening without feeling bad about himself—but I'm afraid there is more to it than that. There is a secondary effect of protecting men from rejection. People who don't experience rejection don't learn to deal with it. It contributes to a culture of entitlement, which in turn creates a bigger problem of harassment.

Sadly, because we've created a culture in which many men don't know how to deal with rejection, sometimes we do have to choose our own safety over honesty. Men seem to respect the fact that we are someone else's property, even when they don't respect our right to say yes or no.

In 2019, eighteen-year-old Gabrielle Walsh was punched in the face so hard that it knocked her unconscious after she told a man outside a Manchester nightclub that she wasn't interested in him. She didn't opt for the feeling-sparing lie; instead, she told the truth. The near-stranger smacked her in the face in response.

Gabrielle Walsh's experience is not an isolated one. Instagrammer Bianca Devins was allegedly murdered by a man whom she rejected romantically. In 2014, Elliot Rodger committed a mass murder near a California university, citing the romantic rejection of multiple women as his reason. Before his death, Rodger wrote a 141-page manifesto in which he expressed his anger toward women who would not have sex with him. In his manifesto, he claimed he intended to target "the kind of girls I've always desired but was never able to have." The list of cases where a woman has refused a man and then paid for it with her life goes on and on and on.

Gabrielle Walsh did the "right" thing when she told a man she wasn't attracted to that she wasn't interested. She did the "rude" thing—the thing that on paper I would cheer her on for doing—but sometimes doing the right thing has horrible consequences.

In a perfect world, all women would stop sugarcoating rejections. There is no reason that we should feel obliged to say we have a boyfriend, that we're too tired, that we're gay or on our way home to see our overprotective spouse instead of telling the truth, but sometimes we have to be pragmatic. Sometimes we have to do the wrong thing for the right reason. Putting a fake diamond on your left ring finger on a night out to avoid giving men the brush-off is pandering, but then sometimes pandering is the safest thing to do. Hopefully, one day, we can create a culture in which men's romantic feelings aren't protected above all else.

If we could raise an entire generation of men who are comfortable with being rejected because a woman isn't attracted to them, not because they've already been claimed by another man, we'd have a much better and safer world. One of the most unhelpful things that we do is teach children that if a boy likes a girl, he will be aggressive or unkind to her, that he will tease her and pull her hair.

In 2015, a mother named Merritt Smith posted a picture of her four-year-old daughter, who had been hit so hard by another child at school that she required stitches. She posted the following statement on Facebook:

"I bet he likes you"

Dear man at the registration desk at Children's hospital, I'm positive that you didn't think that statement through. As soon as I heard it, I knew that is where it begins. That statement is where the idea that hurting is flirting begins to set a tone for what is acceptable behavior. My four-year-old knows, "That's not how we show we like someone." That was not a good choice.

In that moment, [we were] hurt and in a new place,

worried about perhaps getting a shot or stitches [and] you were a person we needed to help us, and your words of comfort conveyed a message that someone who likes you might hurt you. No. I will not allow that message to be ok. I will not allow it to be louder than: "That's not how we show we like each other."

At that desk, you are in a position of influence, whether you realize it or not. You thought you were making the moment lighter. It is time to take responsibility for the messages we as a society give our children. Do not tell my 4-year-old who needs stitches from a boy at school hitting her, "I bet he likes you."

Can we really be surprised that men lash out at the women who reject them if during childhood they are taught that being unkind to women they are romantically interested in is the norm? We can and should raise our sons to be better than that.

When I contacted Merritt to ask her about what she had written, she told me that since her Facebook post had gone viral the staff at the hospital—who were, she assured me, generally great—had been given training in order to avoid other similar comments being made in the future. By refusing to accept these outdated comments, Merritt made a real change.

Danger

When I was twenty-two, I had a date with a man at an expensive London hotel bar. He was an attractive Canadian, in town for work. He implied that he thought I was average-looking but bought me a second cocktail and kept talking. The understanding had been that I was going to go upstairs with him. So, despite the fact that my Spidey senses were screaming, I did. When we got upstairs, I asked him if I could use the bathroom and he said no. I was confused. Something seemed off.

I asked him if I could go back downstairs and use the bathroom there and he got frustrated with me. Something was not right.

When I tell this story people often suggest that maybe he was just embarrassed that he'd left the bathroom a mess. Every instinct I had was screaming that he was a danger to me. So, I ran away. I literally ran, into the hall, down several flights of stairs, through the lobby, and down the Strand. To this day, I rate it as one of the better decisions that I've ever made.

If he was just a sweet man who had a messy bathroom, he was no doubt offended and hurt by my being extremely rude. But in that moment, I shouldn't have been weighing that up. I made a split-second choice that something was off, that my comfort was more important than his feelings, and left, and I made the right decision. The most shocking thing about this story, writing it down half a decade later, is that I considered risking my safety in order to prevent a complete stranger from thinking me rude for letting him buy me cocktails and then running away.

THE RIGHT KIND OF
Rude About Dating

───────────

- ▶ You're not obligated to spare anyone else's feelings. Of course, being nasty for the sake of it achieves nothing, but if you're telling a lie to a stranger, ask yourself why.

- ▶ Just because someone is being abusive via an app rather than in person, it does not mean that you have to ignore it. Dick pics might be a punch line, but it's also cyber flashing, and there is a movement to make it illegal.

- ▶ Sometimes when you avoid being rude to someone you've been on a few dates with, you tell yourself that it's to protect their feelings, when realistically it's to avoid the awkwardness of an honest conversation. This is where you need to be rude for someone else's sake.

- ▶ Ghosting normally happens when you're trying to avoid rudeness. It's the wrong kind of rude. Far better to explain that the chemistry isn't there than to just go silent. Honesty is the right kind of rude.

- ▶ No one "deserves" your romantic attention. You do not owe anyone anything on that front.

- ▶ The exception to every rule when it comes to rude dating is your own safety. If you get a red flag about someone, you have every right to remove yourself from any situation.

ANNE BOLEYN

◀ ▶

Anne Boleyn was born around 1501, though the exact year of her birth is unknown. She died in 1536. She was beheaded on charges of adultery, treason by way of plotting to kill the king, and incest. She is thought to have been accused of witchcraft, though this isn't entered as a formal charge. It might seem odd to pick a rude dating icon who lived centuries before dating even really existed. But, before things went horribly wrong and she was effectively murdered by her husband, Anne played a dating game that came straight out of the *Rude* playbook.

Anne met Henry VIII at the English court while he was still married to his first wife, Catherine of Aragon, who had in turn been married to Henry's brother Arthur until his death. Henry hadn't been a model of fidelity until Anne came along, having had a long relationship with a mistress named Bessie

Blount and a relationship with Anne's sister, Mary (though the seriousness of that relationship depends on which historian you believe). Anne, it seems, was different. Henry broke with the Catholic Church and moved toward Protestantism, at least in part so that he could divorce Catherine of Aragon and marry Anne Boleyn, a move thought to be at least partially inspired by Anne's theological scholarship. Anne's robust self-esteem meant she felt she deserved more.

In a time when women were chattel before marriage and baby incubators afterward, Anne refused to be either. The general consensus by historians is that one of Anne's major skills in becoming a wife rather than a mistress was withholding sex while dangling the prospect of it in front of a man who had never been told no by anyone. It's a tactic that you will genuinely see exhibited (to greater and lesser levels of success) on *The Bachelor*.

Generally speaking, when we talk about Anne Boleyn, who lived far enough back in history for her public perception to be a tangle of fact and fiction, she is portrayed as a seductress. There are schools of thought that she was the original "everything but" girl who engaged in foreplay with Henry, and there are some suggestions that her time growing up at the French court had equipped her with some sexual skills that were unusual for an English lady. Regardless of how much of this is true and how much was invented by her detractors after her death, the point remains: Anne's ability to say no to a man who had never been denied anything before meant that she got what she wanted—and happened to split the British monarchy from the most powerful church in the world. As the old Internet adage goes, Henry VIII broke with Rome to sleep with Anne Boleyn, and you can't even get a text back.

Anne's political astuteness has often been overlooked by history. What is often lost among the rumors of her seduction is the undeniable truth that Anne was intelligent, perceptive, and adept at social politics. As a woman in the sixteenth century, Anne had very little to work with. But she used her intelligence and her cunning in order to make herself into one of the most powerful women in the world—no mean feat indeed.

In 2020, women don't have to dangle sex—withhold sex—in order to advance themselves. And they shouldn't. Sex should been seen as an activity that is enjoyable and pleasurable, not as something to be used as a strategic tool. Sex should be used for fun, not for progress. However, there are still plenty of lessons for us to learn from Anne in terms of modern dating. She knew her worth. She kept her standards sky-high, and she was unwilling to compromise. She wasn't afraid to say no. Anne Boleyn would not get an Uber to someone else's house at three a.m. in order to give a blow job to someone who'd fall asleep straight afterward and look nauseous when she referred to him as her boyfriend. While you're not technically a sixteenth-century British noblewoman, you shouldn't do these things (unless that's what you're into—in that case, go wild!) either.

4 | RUDE
About Sex

Back in 2014, my friend Angelica Malin and I launched an online sex magazine called *About Fucking Time*. Our mission statement was very simple: good sex is a right, not a privilege. We launched the (now defunct) magazine after spending our early twenties listening to our friends talking about their mediocre sex lives and coming to the conclusion that something really had to change. Time and time again, I have listened to women say that they cannot orgasm, that sex isn't really for them, that they only like sex because it makes them feel close to their partner, or that they have sex when they don't feel like it because it's "easier."

If there is once place where being rude makes sense, it's in the bedroom. You strip away every other aspect of societal expectation. You're naked, touching each other, making noises and faces, tasting and smelling each other's bodies. There really shouldn't be any space for a fear of being rude—sex is the rudest thing two people can do. And yet that fear runs rampant, especially among women.

Despite now being the official flag bearer for honesty during sex and demanding at least as much pleasure as you give, I understand why women opt for a Neville Chamberlain–style policy of appeasement during sex, because I spent much of my adult life doing the exact same thing.

When I was eighteen, I started a four-year-long, committed-but-nonexclusive relationship with a man in his fifties. He was incredibly sexually experienced, and while there were other aspects of our relationship that weren't great, he was very generous in bed. However, I was nervous, self-conscious, and struggled to reach orgasm as quickly as I thought I was supposed to. Porn had given me the impression that I should come in less than five minutes, and that anything longer was just plain wrong. So, the first time we had sex, I faked it. And the thing about faking it is that once you start, you have to keep going.

I kept faking orgasms for six months. Occasionally I would allow myself a real orgasm, and he would comment on how much longer it had taken. Not with judgment, just with curiosity, making sure that I was okay, that he hadn't done something I didn't like. Of course, I could have said something, but is there anything ruder than admitting to someone that you've been faking orgasms for months? That their kindly sexual efforts weren't good enough to bring you to climax?

It seemed rude to expect a man to spend twenty minutes helping me to come, and whenever I would get close, I would worry about how long I was taking and lose my groove. So I just skipped the whole party. It didn't occur to me that perhaps this man wouldn't mind giving up twenty minutes of his life to make me come. It also didn't occur to me that I'd spent a lot longer than twenty minutes giving blow jobs and hand jobs and that I might deserve some reciprocal attention. Faking it seemed polite, so that's what I did.

Sex became a performance. The orgasm had to seem real, convincing and satisfying without being over-the-top enough to arouse suspicion. I used to boast at drinks with girlfriends that I was the Meryl Streep of faking orgasms.

Eventually I got older, ballsier, and less generous in the bedroom. My fake orgasms went from Meryl Streep to Lindsay Lohan, and my boyfriend at the time realized what was going on. One day we were having sex; I was on top, and I gave my faux climax a 3 out of 10 on the effort scale. "Darling?" he asked after we finished. "Was that . . . real?"

I dived face-first into the pillows and attempted to mask my bright red face. "No," I said into the pillow. "I faked it."

"Why would you fake it?" he asked me. "Has it happened before? How often?"

So, I did the rude thing and told him the truth. I'd faked the vast majority of the orgasms I had had with him. I also explained that I had done so out of guilt about how long it takes me to orgasm, the stress of not performing properly, and a desire to seem like I was good at sex. It was a painfully embarrassing conversation that I have not enjoyed reliving. But, after that, things got better. I stopped faking. I relaxed, and eventually, I learned the joy of having sex with someone when it's not a race to climax. And it turned out that the grand irony was that once I stopped worrying about how long it took me to reach orgasm, it got a whole lot quicker. Twenty minutes became five, and now I can orgasm with my husband almost as quickly as I can alone. I also realized that even if you don't orgasm during penetrative sex, it's very reasonable to expect to have an orgasm.

My husband is the only person I've ever slept with with whom I've never faked an orgasm. Perhaps that is a sign. But our gratifying sex life is due, at least in part, to my rudeness.

When we first started sleeping together, my husband had recently gotten out of a long-term relationship. I quite quickly realized that he still had a sex routine that had been honed on someone else's body. The entire thing had been designed between two people and probably worked for them, but parts of it didn't work for me, and the idea that he was applying someone else's likes and dislikes to me made me feel uncomfortable.

Had I been sensible I would have said, "I don't like the way that feels," or "Could you do that harder?" But instead I tried time and time again to give him nonverbal cues. I'd wiggle in one direction for yes and another for no. Make noises like I was trying to give him echolocation. But in the end, I realized that it wasn't going to work. He was not going to magically figure out—especially as we'd only been sleeping together a couple of weeks—what was working for me. So I told him. It was embarrassing and hard, and I felt ungrateful, but I told him everything he was doing that didn't work. And I did it using a classic management tactic: you give a compliment, then a criticism, then another compliment.

Being rude doesn't have to mean being nasty. It's perfectly fine to say, "I love it when you kiss my neck, but when you bite me it makes me feel uncomfortable." Of course, there is nothing wrong with being totally blunt; let's be honest, when you've seen each other's assholes, there's really no need to be coy. It is all about finding the level of rude that is comfortable for you. If you need to feed someone a compliment sandwich in order to say the rude thing you've been avoiding, you do you. Baby steps and all that.

Tell the men you sleep with that your orgasm matters. Point it out if they are not pleasing you sexually. Don't lie there with your legs open letting someone prod at your arid clitoris or pull at your nipples because they are a nice person or because you think it's just part of having casual sex. It's not. There is no point in having sex unless you are going to enjoy it.

The Orgasm Gap

A study published in the *Archives of Sexual Behavior* in 2017 found that straight women have fewer orgasms at the hands of their partners than any other group. Unlike lesbian women, who reported always or almost always achieving orgasm during sex, women who stuck to male partners only reported having orgasms around 65 percent of the time. On the other hand, 95 percent of men reported that they always or almost always orgasm during sex.

Some other (quite depressing) facts about the female orgasm, from a 2017 Family Planning Association study that was open to women of any age and any sexual orientation:

- Over 80 percent of women could not reach orgasm through intercourse
- Most women (72 percent) reported difficulty in achieving a simultaneous orgasm with their partners
- About one in seven women had experienced pain during orgasm
- Almost 3 percent of the women had never had an orgasm

And according to Public Health England, 42 percent of women would describe their sex life as "unsatisfactory." Isn't that just brilliant? Almost half of us are having unsatisfactory sex.

In 2019, when I was running the *Grazia* UK website, I asked the women who worked for me to tell me their most controversial opinion as part of a features meeting. They ranged from the amusing to the bizarre. A writer named Georgia Aspinall told me, "I think penetrative sex is a scam." We all laughed, but when she wrote the piece, I realized how right she is. Unless you're trying to get pregnant, there really isn't any point in being penetrated with a penis. You can orgasm without it, you can use toys to simulate it, you can still enjoy a mutually gratifying sex life with your partner without it. Most women don't orgasm from penetration anyway. The fact that we say "sex" and think "penetration" perfectly demonstrates how little women's pleasure is centered in the conversation about sex. While I'd never tell anyone else how to run their sex life, I have taken Georgia's advice and slightly refocused my sex life to include more sex that is about mutual enjoyment and less that is solely about penetration.

Saying No

There is a very old, very incorrect concept that men like sex more than women do—that men enjoy sex and that women provide it as a service. That isn't the case. A 2019 study of two thousand people, undertaken by IllicitEncounters.com, found that 43 percent of women said they had a higher libido than the person that they're sleeping with, while 42 percent of men said the same thing. So, on average, we're all as horny as each other, but as the previous statistics show, women's libidos are less often satisfied during their sexual encounters.

Anyway, the idea of women not liking sex has long, complicated roots in history, politics, and religion. Suffice it to say, it was convenient to create a myth that women do not like or want sex and that men need to trick, convince, or bribe them into having it.

Women were taught to say no if they weren't married. However, they were rarely taught that they were allowed to say no after marriage. Shockingly, until 1991, marital rape was not a crime in the UK. Women weren't supposed to say no to their husbands because sex was considered to be part of their wifely duty.

Depressingly, a 2018 YouGov survey of four thousand people commissioned by the End Violence Against Women Coalition revealed that one in four Britons believed that non-consensual sex within marriage did not constitute rape. Even if you're not in the terrifying 25 percent who believe that marital rape doesn't exist, there is still a stigma about saying no to sex when you're in a relationship. Jokes about women "having a headache" or automatically going off sex the moment they get married speak of a wider cultural expectation that women aren't sexual in their own right and therefore are likely to deliberately withhold sex from their partners.

Saying no to sex should have absolutely no emotional, logistical, or social repercussions. Your partner should not seem hurt, frustrated, annoyed, or resentful if you don't want sex. Of course they are fully entitled to ask for a discussion if your sex life takes an active downturn, but even then, the understanding should not be that sex is an obligation, and the emphasis should be, "I miss having sex with you—has something changed and can I help to alleviate those changes?" not "Why won't you have sex with me anymore?"

Part of the problem is the fact that we all think that everyone else is having more sex than they actually are. As part of a study on misperceptions, which became a book titled *The Perils of Perception*, the research agency Ipsos asked people in Britain and the US to guess how often people aged eighteen to twenty-nine in their country had had sex in the previous four weeks. The average guess about young men in both countries was that they'd had sex fourteen times in the last month. In reality, the actual number was just five in Britain and four in the US.

The perception that everyone else is constantly getting laid contributes to the pressure to never say no to sex. But the problem is, if you say yes to sex that you don't want, the sex will probably be mediocre. Which makes you feel less inclined to have sex next time and probably makes your partner feel pretty lousy too. If, instead, you stop worrying about being rude, say, "Not tonight, darling," and wait until you're feeling really horny to jump your partner's bones, then your sex life will improve. Stop measuring how great your sex life is by how often you do it and start measuring it by how satisfied you are and how much fun you're having.

Condoms, Stealthing, and the Law

We discuss condoms more fully in the "Rude About Health" chapter. Suffice it to say, many men complain about condoms, while many women find them a better and more practical way to have safe sex.

I've never understood the temptation to forgo the condom. Yes, it might feel better, but you know what doesn't feel great? Thinking you might be carrying the child of a man named Andre who you're pretty sure took $20 from your wallet on the way out. Neither, I am reliably informed, does having to spend a day waiting at a clinic because you've got a worrying itch. There's nothing wrong with an unplanned pregnancy or catching an STI, but if you can avoid either of them, then you might as well. And yet, despite the very solid logic behind using condoms, men will fight to avoid them.

One of my first experiences of trying to be rude during sex was when I was at college. After a drunken party, I fell into bed with a very attractive and very cocky guy whom I quite liked. Before we started having sex, I handed him a condom. "Do we have to?" he asked. "I don't have anything." He didn't even ask if I did. For all he knew I could have been riddled with previously undiscovered vaginal woes. "Yes, we do," I insisted.

The sex was fine—nothing to write home about—but then a little way into the drunken fumbling I noticed him starting to take off the condom. "I'm sorry, what are you doing?" I asked in shock.

"It's annoying me," he told me. Without thinking about it, I got another condom from the bedside table and handed it to him. Begrudgingly, he put it on. Later the same thing happened; I saw him reaching to take the condom off, and only when I looked him in the eye and said, "You know I'm not on the pill?" did he keep the damn thing on.

I should not have had to terrify a man with the prospect of fathering my child in order for him to keep the condom on. I also should have felt that the moment he tried to take the condom off, therefore taking us from consenting condom sex to nonconsenting unprotected sex, I could tell him to fuck off. But I didn't. A big part of me was flattered that he was interested in sleeping with me. And on top of that, I felt like I was being boring for forcing him to wear a condom, like I was a big killjoy who wasn't cool or adult enough to be on the pill. So I didn't shout down his total lack of respect for my boundaries. I waited until he had his orgasm—needless to say, I did not have one— and then tried to sleep in a way so as not to disturb him.

Anal, Facials, and Kink

The British Sexual Fantasy Research Project claims that 62 percent of Brits have had a fantasy about being either dominant or submissive in the bedroom. They also found that around 2.2 million Brits admit that they've had violent sexual fantasies. One in five women between the ages of twenty and thirty-nine had anal sex in 2010, and 46 percent have tried it at least once, compared with just 33 percent in 1992. In short, we're increasingly a nation of kinky bastards. And that's absolutely fine. As long as it is consensual.

Unfortunately, that isn't always the case. Over and over again I speak to women who've gone home with guys after dates, absolutely expecting sex. But not the kind of sex they're getting. Instead, without any negotiation or discussion, the guy they're with tries to spank them. Or tries to have anal sex without asking. Or slaps them across the face. Or chokes them (something you really shouldn't try unless you've done the research first).

There's no shame at all in wanting to have rough or kinky sex, but without prearranged negotiation you've basically taken a woman home with you and then smacked her around. It is easy to say that women should just say no if they don't want to, but, in the heat of the moment, doing so is hard. And in the age of increasingly kinky porn, it's easy to feel that you're a big boring prude for preferring a man to come inside you rather than on your face while holding a hunk of your hair.

Every time I've had a man do something to me sexually that I wasn't in the mood for, or that I judged a bit risky, I know they would have stopped if I'd told them to. I've often had sex where there has been a safe word for that exact purpose. But the thing is, saying the safe word (or in less kinky sex, just saying, "I don't think I'm up for that") takes huge confidence. It's rejecting someone when they're being vulnerable toward you; it's declaring yourself as not being up for specific sexual acts. Sometimes it kills the mood. Which is why so many of us have put up with being fishhooked or had painful anal sex.

If you are someone who enjoys kinkier or rougher sex, learning to safe-word is essential, even though it can be difficult. Some people prefer to have a nonverbal safe word, such as a movement or hand gesture, which can feel easier to make than saying a word out loud. Other people find that using the other person's first name, rather than a specific word, makes safe-wording easier.

The same acts that are gratifying when you find them enjoyable are abusive or degrading when you don't want or enjoy them. And yet we choose that degradation over the other, apparently less appealing option of saying: "We didn't discuss doing this and it's making me feel uncomfortable, I'd like to stop." Even in the moment when we're facedown with our buttholes on display, we still cannot bring ourselves to be rude.

Another essential part of enjoying more complex sexual activities in a safe way is the negotiation. All kinky activities should be discussed and agreed on beforehand. Some couples go so far as to fill out a full spreadsheet of activities with a yes, no, or maybe next to them. That contract negotiation scene in *Fifty Shades of Grey* might have seemed funny on paper, but it's something that people really do. And yes, it can feel really silly when you're doing it, but it helps protect against accidentally getting things wrong. Plus, it's extremely liberating to let someone know all of the activities in the bedroom that you would really like to have them do to you, while also making clear where the big red flags are.

Sex Out of Politeness

As a result of the #MeToo movement, a conversation has started to emerge about sexual gray areas. And many women have started to talk openly about the fact that lots of us have had sex not through force, not even through coercion, but through politeness. Of the women who took the *Rude* survey, 58 percent of them said that they had at some point in their life had sex out of politeness. Many respondents answered that they had done this many times. A few even said that they had had sex out of politeness almost every time that they had done it.

Back in 2017 I wrote an article titled "Women Are Having Sex Out of Politeness and That's Got to Stop." It's one of the things I've been most contacted about in the course of my career. Hundreds of women messaged me to tell me that I wasn't the only one who had had sex out of politeness.

My ultimate politeness sex story goes like this: In my late teens I had dinner with a middle-aged couple I didn't know well. I had met them through a wider group of friends, and they were friendly, nice. The woman asked me to dinner, and I said yes. Two weeks later I was sitting in their kitchen.

The wife made a curry. It was probably lovely, but it was way too hot for me (I have the palate of a small baby). Every bite I took hurt my mouth, but I didn't want to be rude. So, I said nothing and I ate it. They probably had Greek yogurt in the fridge. I could have just eaten the rice. There were easy fixes, ways to stop burning my tongue without offending anyone, but I didn't say anything. Because I didn't want to be rude.

After the curry, we went upstairs and had a threesome, also because I didn't want to be rude. I wasn't that attracted to her and I really wasn't attracted to her husband, but they'd been so nice to me—they'd made me dinner, after all! Plus, we'd flirted a bit in the kitchen. It wasn't like they hadn't been dropping hints.

Anyway, while I'd enjoyed the flirting and maybe even liked the idea of having a threesome, I definitely didn't want to have a threesome with them. Which was how I found myself lying on the bed, my eyes very tightly shut, trying to focus on the fact that this, like all things, would end. Telling myself that it would be awkward to ask them to stop, that I'd come this far so I might as well just get on with it. Afterward I smiled a lot and said that I'd had fun. The woman told her husband to walk me back to the tube with their dog, which he clearly didn't want to do. I lied and said I was going to get a taxi home.

Isn't that amazing? The man I'd just had a threesome with didn't really want to go out into the cold, so when his wife suggested he walk me to the tube, he honestly replied, "I don't really want to." He didn't toy with it, wrestle with it, struggle with it; he just said it.

The threesome wasn't a fun night, but it wasn't a traumatic experience either. I don't think of it that often. But I didn't enjoy it. And if I could go back in time and un–sleep with them, I probably would. I like to think that with ten years' more experience I would be able to mention before I arrived that I don't do well with spicy food, and, once I got there, I also could say that I'm not really into the idea of a threesome, either.

THE RIGHT KIND OF
Rude About Sex

▶ Faking an orgasm is a personal choice. You should not feel guilty about faking or about refusing to fake. Instead you should pick whichever serves your own purpose best and roll with it.

▶ However, in a long-term relationship, if you're not enjoying sex, you need to have that conversation. Sex should not be a service that you are providing for another person.

▶ Only a tiny, tiny percentage of women is actually incapable of orgasming. If you are struggling, you might need time, a change of tack, or to double down on your efforts solo. Don't just accept that you don't come and live without orgasms.

▶ By the time you're getting naked with someone, you should be comfortable enough to also be able to tell them what you want or need in the bedroom.

▶ Having sex doesn't have to mean penetration. You can set the boundaries about who puts what where, and those boundaries can be different every single time.

▶ You are never, ever obligated to have sex with another person unless you want to. You can be as rude as you like in order to ensure that it does not happen.

▶ As the person who will initially bear the brunt of contraceptive failure, contraceptive choices are up to you. If the person whom you are having sex with objects to using a condom, then you should object to sleeping with them. When given the choice between condommed sex and no sex at all, the choice is usually quite an easy one.

▶ If you change your mind partway through a sexual encounter, you're perfectly within your rights to get up, put your clothes on, and leave. No one else's right to have sex is more important than your right to choose whom you have sex with and when.

LADY IDINA SACKVILLE

◀ ▶

Lady Myra Idina Sackville was born in Sussex in 1893 and died in Kenya in 1955. She married and divorced five times, which earned her the nickname "the Bolter." She was used as the inspiration for a character in several books by Nancy Mitford, and her name was synonymous with scandal in British society. At a time when sex was widely considered to be a slightly unpleasant wifely duty that took place at a husband's behest, Idina demonstrated a thirst for pleasure, exploration, and adventure, which included a voracious sexual appetite.

After divorcing her first husband and leaving him with her two sons, something that would be scandalous in 2020, let alone in 1924, she moved to Kenya and married Captain Charles Gordon. She then took a lover, Joss Hay, whom she in turn eventually married. Much of Idina's adulthood was spent living in the Happy Valley, an area of Kenya where a group of British expatriates enjoyed a life of sex, drugs, and near-constant socializing. At the height of her fun she would throw parties and greet guests naked in a green onyx bathtub before dressing in front of them. During dinner, she would encourage the swapping of room keys—which unsurprisingly ended in the swapping of partners.

Idina's biographer, Frances Osborne, found out only when she was in her late teens that she was the great-granddaughter of "the Bolter." When she asked her parents why they had kept it a secret, they told her that they were worried she might see Idina as some kind of role model.

There are plenty of objectionable actions among Idina's life choices. She didn't raise any of her three children herself. She allegedly broke the hearts of many of the men she had relationships with or married. But one area in which she cannot be faulted is her lack of shame.

Aside from "the Bolter," the word most used to describe Idina is "shameless." Originally this would have been intended as an insult, because Edwardian society was based on a hearty sense of shame around most pleasurable things. But Idina didn't play that way. Instead she indulged her desires.

Arguably, much of her scandalous or unkind behavior wasn't caused by her own selfishness, but rather the fact that it wasn't possible to be both a dutiful wife and mother and someone who enjoyed a varied sex life.

Luckily the world is somewhat different now. While there is still plenty of shame associated with sex, especially having lots of sex with lots of different people, women are increasingly acting upon their desires openly and boldly.

I would encourage anyone who finds themselves putting up with a mediocre sex life to think of Lady Idina Sackville and of the enormous sacrifices she made in order to be able to have exciting sex. Perhaps on some level we owe it to bold, brave, disruptive women like her not to make do with a mediocre sex life, but rather to embrace our rudeness and refuse to be ashamed of our desires.

5 | RUDE
About
Weddings

If you want to see a woman in her late twenties or early thirties lose the will to live, ask her to add up how much she has spent on attending other people's weddings in recent years. The light will drain out from her eyes as she mentally adds up just how much of her hard-earned cash has gone to dresses, hotel rooms, rental cars, drinks from the cash bars, and goddamn presents for couples who are already having enormous parties and then going on the fanciest vacations of their lives. Not to mention the fact that if you're part of the bridal party, you'll be expected to go to the bachelorette party, a phenomenon that, in recent years, has gone from meaning a sloppy night out at the club to, in many cases, an entire weekend spent in some far-flung locale. Oh, and I'm forgetting the bridal shower!

It is a truth universally acknowledged that between the ages of about twenty-six and thirty-six, you will spend the majority of your summers and your salary traveling to remote parts of the country and paying through the nose to sleep in questionable Airbnbs because your boyfriend's work friend is getting married, your cousin is getting married, a girl you went to college with is getting married.

Lots of us find that the first couple of weddings we attend are exciting because they're gloriously novel, but by the time we've been to a few per summer, the joy is gone. I, on the other hand, find that the more I embrace my rudeness, the more I am able to enjoy weddings. This year I haven't used up all my nuptial goodwill on going to every single wedding in the Western Hemisphere and bankrupting myself in the process, but instead have reserved my very genuine joy for the weddings I *am* attending, and I haven't cost couples I barely know $100 a plate.

I used to write a column called "Modern Etiquette." The vast majority of the questions that I got were wedding related, because weddings dominate so much of our free time and eat up so much of our income. There is this sense that the wants and needs of a couple getting married absolutely come first, even if that means you run out of vacation time, put strain on your credit card, or pay through the nose to do activities that make your toes curl.

This chapter started life as a little note in the friendship section, but the more I wrote, the more it became clear that weddings are one of the areas where we all need a kick up the ass in learning to be rude, because it's totally possible to protect your annual vacation time and life savings without being a bitch.

If you're wondering where to start in terms of trying out positive rudeness, then the next wedding invitation that you receive will provide the perfect test ground.

Saying No

The envelope drops onto your doormat. Once, a long, long time ago, you might have been excited at the prospect of a weekend away, but now the invitation comes with a healthy side of dread. Rather than putting it on the mantelpiece and looking at it with a glower of resentment every day for three months, do something revolutionary: Decide whether you actually want to go. If you're sure that you don't want to go, then RSVP no.

It's easy to think that because weddings tend to be planned a long way in advance that you can't say no. This is bullshit. It's an invitation, not a summons. "No" is a complete sentence, and if you've been invited to the wedding of someone you don't like enough to want to watch them get married, then it doesn't really matter if they're a bit miffed that you don't want to attend their special day. Though to be honest, if they're significantly bothered about your RSVP, then they're clearly not that diverted by the whole "happiest day of your life" thing. "Dear Rachel, thank you for your very kind invitation; sadly I won't be able to join you, but I'm wishing you every happiness." Bam. Saturday the first of June is now yours in which to watch Netflix and pluck your toe hairs, all because you were bold enough to be the right kind of rude.

All of this is easier said than done. I used to have a horrible tendency to say yes to an invitation, assuming that I would be more open to the idea of going closer to the time. Of course, that was complete nonsense. If an event is unappealing the day you receive the invitation, it will still be unappealing down the line. My truly charming habit is to dread said event, worry about it, wait until it gets really close, and then pretend to be ill. This is the wrong kind of rude. It's thoughtless, it inconveniences other people, and it leaves me feeling horribly guilty. All in all, to be avoided. (For clarification, I have never done this for a wedding, though I have been sorely tempted.)

If you do want to go to the wedding (or any other social occasion), then work out how much you're willing to spend on it. It's okay that you probably have a different budget in mind for a close friend's wedding in a lovely location than you have for your third cousin's handfasting in a terrible town on the other side of the country. The couple is never going to know that you did a cost-benefit analysis about going to their special day. There are some people—close friends, family members— whom you should make an effort for. But you've got limited time, money, and energy to spend, so you can't be wasting those precious resources on a wedding where, to be perfectly honest, the couple would probably hardly notice whether you were there or not.

Presents

One of the first weddings I ever attended was quite a lavish affair for a couple who had plenty of money. The day before the ceremony I remembered, with gut-twisting panic, that I hadn't bought them a present—a big faux pas for a British wedding. Of course, when I logged on to their registry the only things left were disgustingly expensive. I was making minimum wage as a receptionist and I almost cried as I spent a day's pay on a bathroom trash can for them. Why? You probably know the answer by now. I didn't want to be rude.

It's not rude to keep your spending within a comfortable limit. You did not choose to invite yourself to the wedding, nor did you force the happy couple to cater steak for a hundred people. Therefore, it is not your responsibility to offset their costs for the wedding via gifting. If you want to buy a present, then that's lovely. But if it's going to cause you stress, make your life harder, or put you into debt, then absolutely fuck that. Your friends do not need copper-topped salt-and-pepper grinders more than you need to be able to pay your electricity bill.

Taking a card shows that you thought about it, rather than forgot entirely. If you want to give a gift but you're not feeling flush, there's nothing wrong with going a bit homespun. I gave some friends who had a nine-year-old daughter two date nights of free babysitting when they got married. I got to know their daughter, they got cheap childcare, and I didn't spend $75 on a hand towel.

Plus-Ones

The only thing more annoying than traveling halfway across the country to eat a mass-produced roast dinner in celebration of someone else's relationship is doing it alone. If you've got a plus-one, then you can at least split the cost of a hotel room and have a glorious bitch about the bridesmaids' dresses after the whole thing wraps up. Of course, the person throwing the wedding might not want to give you a plus-one. From the engaged couple's point of view, unless they know both halves of the couple equally well, a plus-one is a waste. They're paying for dinner and drinks for a complete stranger. Which is why you often find that you're invited to a wedding solo. The "no ring, no bring" policy is massively popular—even Kate and William employed it for their royal wedding, which probably had more to do with space limitations than cost. But anyway, the plus-one policy around weddings is largely constructed around how serious you and your other half are, and if you're single, then you can dream on.

It would be rude to tell the happy couple that you'd only like to attend if you can bring a plus-one, but it's also kind of rude that you're only allowed to bring a guest if you're in a long-term romantic relationship. Of course, if it's a huge wedding full of people whom you know and love, then it's fine, but if you only know a handful of people, isn't it worth being rude, asking for a guest, and circumventing a situation where you spend $400 to make forced conversation with strangers? The bride and groom would be totally within their rights to tell you that they don't want to give you a plus-one because they don't have the space or budget. You would be entirely within your rights to decide that if you don't have a plus-one, you don't need to go.

A word to the wise: if you're going to have this conversation, especially in a world where being honest about your feelings is still quite a new concept, it's better to do it face-to-face. When we discuss things in writing, all the nuance is lost, and the tone disappears. You can't read a reaction and temper the strength of your phrasing to meet the needs of the room. It's why arguments online or over email are so much more toxic than when they are face-to-face. Telling your friend to her face "I'm so happy for you, but it's a lot of money and vacation time to come and sit on my own at the singles' table" is less likely to go as badly as a WhatsApp message saying "I'm only coming if I can bring someone" will.

Also, it's much harder to say no to someone's face. Saying no to an email just means typing whatever you want to say, hitting send, and then slamming your screen shut and pretending nothing happened. Whereas looking someone in the eye and telling them that they can't have something they want is far, far harder.

For a long time, I knew this to be true, and that was why I decided to make requests via email or message, so that anyone who said yes to me was doing so because they really wanted to. Which is admirable but not very effective. If you want something that someone isn't keen to give you—time off work during a busy period, a salary raise, a plus-one to a wedding—and you believe that they should give it to you, then you should, if possible, ask in person.

It's something that I still struggle with. I, like a lot of

women, consider my wants and needs to be less important than everyone else's. So I self-sabotage by making requests in a way that makes it easy for the answer to be no. But that's pointless. If a request is reasonable enough that you feel confident in making it, then you should have the courage of your convictions and ask in the way that is most likely to get the yes.

Bachelorette Parties

I recently girded my loins and transferred $270 to a demi-friend, and as I typed "Bachelorette party!" into the transaction description box, I couldn't help but wonder why I was paying a large chunk of my weekly living budget to take a bus for six hours to celebrate with someone whom I am ambivalent about. The difficulty about bachelorette parties is that it means handing over a large sum of cash and some of your vacation days, sometimes to a stranger, and hoping that they've got the same concept of a good time that you do. Best-case scenario: you have a brilliant weekend and it was worth the money. Worst-case scenario: you end up spending loads of money to be trapped in the middle of nowhere with a group of people you barely like, with no escape.

According to a study by Hotels.com, the average UK-based bachelor or bachelorette party costs $608 to attend. The average one abroad is $1,229. If you go to four in a year you've spent between $2,400 and $4,900. The average UK salary is $35,717. So, you're paying between 7 and 14 percent of your annual income on making flower crowns and pretending not to feel uncomfortable about the stripper.

Bachelorette-party policy is much the same as wedding policy. Don't say yes unless you actually want to go, and if you do actually want to go, make sure that you can afford it. Don't get yourself into debt or leave yourself in financial stress in order to drink warm prosecco and play pin the cock on the poster. No decent friend will resent you for saying you can't afford to attend, especially if you're open about why. The desire to pretend that you can afford things is very often based in a bigger desire not to make anyone else uncomfortable by being honest about your finances. But if we all got a bit better about admitting when something is too expensive for us, then we'd finally break the emperor's-new-clothes effect.

Bridesmaids

Picture the scene. Your newly engaged friend asks you to meet her for a drink at an expensive cocktail bar quite a long way from your house. When you arrive, she hands you a multicolored card box and inside is a balloon reading, "Will you be my bridesmaid?" It's happened. You friend has been invaded by Pinterest and is now a semi-sentient being who lives to plan her wedding and expects you to care about her nuptials as much as she does. Which is hard because you probably can't imagine caring about your own wedding as much as she wants you to care about her napkin choices.

Bitching about being a bridesmaid is pedestrian and obvious and yet almost impossible to resist. It's not the bride's fault that she's obsessed with the party she's throwing—she's spending her money and every second of free time in the year leading up to it trying to make it lovely.

When I wrote my etiquette column, the single most repeated question was whether or not you can say no to being a bridesmaid. Whether it's because the person who's asked you is too new of a friend for you to feel comfortable, or because you've already done it so many times that the sight of a slip dress in a muted pastel silk makes you want to throw up, the answer is yes. You are allowed to say no to being a bridesmaid. And if you want to say no, you should. It is a far, far, far better thing to say no when you're asked than to say yes and do a subpar job. Friendships can be ruined by saying yes to being a bridesmaid when you wanted to say no.

Carrie, thirty-four, didn't say no to a bridesmaiding gig and still regrets it. "She was a really nice woman from my book club, and I liked her a lot, but we weren't close. I was surprised but flattered to be asked. I hadn't been a bridesmaid many times before, so I wasn't really aware of how much work it was going to be. She wanted an elaborate [bachelorette party] with multiple strippers, a classy sit-down meal, and then a night out in a club, but she wanted it to cost no more than fifty pounds [sixty dollars] a head. I did my absolute best, but I'm an accountant, not a wizard, and I could tell that she thought I was failing. Plus, I soon got pregnant, and bridesmaid responsibilities were just too much to handle on top of a really difficult pregnancy. I told my friend I could no longer be a bridesmaid and take care of myself the way I needed to. It went down really badly. At the wedding there was lots of 'Is that her?' from her other friends. I sent her a stupidly overgenerous present to try to make up for it, but honestly, I should have just had the courage to tell her at the start that I had a child—and another on the way—a job, and no time to help her plan."

Saying no might be badly received at the time, but dropping out of your bridesmaid role halfway through the wedding planning will go down a whole lot worse.

Bridezillas

All of the above might lead you to assume that I'm anti-bridezilla. But, despite the fact that I think it is absolutely okay for you to say no to a couple's (often insane) requests, I also have a whole lot of sympathy for bridezillas who want to make a very big day a very big success. My advice? To attempt to be a kind of bridezilla lite, so you don't spend your life savings on a subpar wedding but you also have some friends left when you get back from your honeymoon.

When we were planning our wedding, my husband and I got into a routine. On a Saturday morning we would get in the car and drive to the florist, the wedding planner, the cake baker, whoever. We would scream at each other for the entirety of the car journey (me because I felt that he didn't care about what type of candles we were having, him because he felt I should pay more heed to speed limits on country lanes), then we would pull up at whatever wedding purveyor we had driven across the country to meet, I would check my lipstick in the rearview mirror, and we'd knock on the front door holding hands and smiling. During the viewing or tasting or whatever it was we were spending our Saturday doing, I would affect an air of sweet relaxation, as if I could hardly believe I was going to have a wedding at all, let alone make emphatic judgments about cake. "What do you think, darling?" I would ask my husband every thirty seconds. I was determined not to be regarded as a bridezilla. It was the bridal version of "I'm not like other girls."

Often, the one time that women are freely rude, demanding, and specific in their wants is when they are getting married. It's because we've been taught since childhood that our wedding will be the zenith of our lives. All of the normal rules that subjugate women seem to expire when we're planning our weddings. Bridezillas aren't born, they're made. But there's a reason why even the most grounded and down-to-earth woman can find herself roaring the words "It's my one special day and I want to feel like a princess." Bridezilla behavior is born of two things: repression and expectation.

I got married at age twenty-six, at which point I'd spent years suppressing my own desires, pretending that I didn't have strong feelings about where I went on vacation or what we had for dinner, saying, "I don't care which restaurant we go to," and then having crippling IBS because my pathetic body can't handle Indian food. But when I got engaged, people seemed to expect me to behave like a control freak—it was my *wedding*, after all. Apparently, because I'd managed to hook myself a man, I was allowed to unleash all the finicky, irrational, gloriously selfish opinions that I'd been repressing since childhood. People who would have been shocked if I'd refused to go for expensive drinks on the other side of London on a Tuesday night were suddenly totally happy to indulge me when I cried over a rumored peony shortage. It felt absolutely fucking great.

Despite the fact that most women have never planned a large-scale event, every wedding I've been to has been a masterstroke of organization almost exclusively created by the female partner. It's a testament to how much we are able to get done when we're freed from the shackles of niceness. When I see female friends turning into bridezillas, it fills me with joy. It's proof that we have it in us. When we feel that we have permission to be assertive, specific, demanding, and selfish, we can create something incredible from a standing start.

The word "bridezilla" belongs on the long list of words that are only ever applied to women, or which have no male equivalent in general usage, and it is of course designed to vilify women during a high-stress period of their lives. But I see the word as an enormous compliment. A bridezilla is a woman who has decided that if she's going to spend all of her savings on a one-day-long party, she's sure as fuck going to have the correct-colored tablecloths. I wish more women were bridezillas in their day-to-day lives—we'd get a lot more done if we just started demanding what we want and making sure we get it. Unfortunately, though, most of us feel that this behavior can only be applied to our wedding day.

THE RIGHT KIND OF
Rude About Weddings

▶ Repeat after me: "It is an invitation, not a summons." Just because you get a lot of notice about it doesn't mean you are obligated to go.

▶ Saying no doesn't mean you have to give an explanation. "Thank you so much but we can't make it" is a complete sentence.

▶ Weddings are supposed to be full of joy. It is far, far worse to go to a wedding with bad grace and resent being there than it is to RSVP saying that you can't come.

▶ Sometimes weddings are only fun if you can have a plus-one. You are not being selfish or horrible for asking if you can bring someone, especially if you don't know anyone else who is going.

▶ If you don't want to attend the wedding without a plus-one, that's okay. The bride and groom get to set their plus-one policy, and you get to decide whether or not you want to attend.

▶ Wedding blindness is a thing. When you're planning a wedding, the shutters come down and you forget that there is anything else going on in the world. Sometimes you need your good friends to risk your wrath and remind you of that fact.

- ▶ Your wedding is a nice party and the start of a marriage; it is not the UN summit on ending climate change. Other people will care about your wedding around 5 percent as much as you would like them to care.
- ▶ The average wedding costs $481 to attend in total. That's practically a vacation. Are you going to have more fun at this wedding than you would on a vacation?
- ▶ You do not need to buy an expensive gift. Picking something cheap from the registry is fine—there is a reason that couples include gifts of all sizes. Alternatively, a framed photo of a happy memory, a thoughtful letter, or a promise for the future is also lovely. Anyone who spends their honeymoon raging that you got them a cheap gift is in the wrong relationship.

SARAH CHURCHILL

◄ ►

Sarah Churchill, Duchess of Marlborough, was born on May 29, 1660, and died October 18, 1744. She was an English courtier who rose to be one of the most influential women of her time through her close friendship with Queen Anne.

If you know anything about Sarah, the chances are that you know it from *The Favourite*, a film about the complex relationship between Queen Anne, Sarah Churchill, and Baroness Masham. While the film obviously wasn't a documentary, much of what it represented, at least in terms of rudeness, was accurate. Queen Anne was (like most monarchs) surrounded by people whom she paid. These people were therefore largely unwilling to tell her unpalatable truths. British monarchs believed—possibly still do believe—in a principle called "the divine right of kings," which meant that any ruling monarch was chosen by God specifically to be his representative on earth. Therefore, telling off the king or the queen was tantamount to telling off God. Add this to the fact that monarchs could have you banished, imprisoned, or killed, and it isn't altogether surprising that people weren't falling over themselves to call out problematic regal behavior.

Sarah's skill as a courtier, aside from her being witty and charming and clever, was that she was also direct, sharp, and (you probably saw this one coming) rude. She famously didn't offer the queen flattery and even still referred to her by her childhood nickname, Mrs. Morley. This was a sort of considered, constructive rudeness that worked incredibly well—for the most part.

For several decades, their friendship flourished. Sarah Churchill held the positions of mistress of the robes and groom of the stool—the two highest positions that a woman could hold. Her husband was promoted and given £7,000 a year from the crown, which is the equivalent of about $925,000 now. Plus, the queen gifted Churchill Blenheim Palace, which has a two-thousand acre estate and 187 rooms.

Unfortunately, Churchill's rudeness did not serve her so well for the rest of her political career. Eventually, her cousin Abigail Hill pitched up at court and decided to take the opposite tack from Churchill, opting to be flattering, supportive, and kind to the queen at all times, regardless of what actually needed to be said or done. Unsurprisingly, this won her more favor than Sarah's brand of efficient political brutality.

In 1707 Abigail was married to Samuel Masham in a secret wedding. The fact that the queen was invited to, and attended, the wedding while Sarah Churchill only learned of it after the fact led to a conversation that wouldn't be out of place in a 2020 WhatsApp group.

Sarah was angered by her exclusion and realized that Masham had become close to the queen without telling Churchill. Having the queen show up at your very small, private wedding was a big deal and a signifier of an extremely close friendship. Plus, as a generous wedding present, the queen gave the Mashams two thousand guineas from the privy purse (the royal budget), which works out to about $274,000. Unsurprisingly, Churchill was angry at her exclusion, but unfortunately she was unable to modulate her rudeness, and as such she fell further from favor and eventually was stripped of her roles. She and her husband left court, building came to a halt on Blenheim Palace, and they retired instead to Germany, where they remained until the queen's death, at which point they returned to England.

Depressingly, not that much has changed since the 1700s, though on the upside, if you don't get invited to a friend's wedding it's unlikely to be a precursor to being banished to another country. Even still, though, as women, it remains difficult to navigate the social minefield of weddings.

Sarah Churchill was perhaps rude beyond what was pragmatic for the time, and unable to rein in her more bullish tendencies, but we would still do well to observe her skill. Her rudeness, tempered with astute political decision-making and charm, led her to be the second-most powerful woman in the country. That is, until a wedding ruined everything for her.

6 | **RUDE**
as a
Consumer

The place where you are most likely to need to learn to be rude on a day-to-day basis is as a customer. Sometimes things just go wrong. Products break, appointments are canceled, the eyebrow threader slips and leaves your face partially bald. The temptation, if you're not a fully paid-up member of the rude club, is to pretend that you are happy to have spent money on something substandard and then go home and complain to people who can do nothing about the situation. We all know this is pointless, and it's time to stop.

The most experience that I've ever had of people being rude—both in a positive and a negative sense—was when I

worked at a very fancy London department store. We were required to wear suits and a full face of makeup, high heels and
a smile, which masked the fact that the high heels were slowly
lacerating our feet. Our job wasn't just to sell things; it was to
make the customer feel so special that she didn't resent how
much money she had spent on something that she could almost
certainly have bought cheaper elsewhere.

There were two types of customers, and while I didn't realize it at the time, they would become the bedrock of my opinions about rudeness.

We had customers who were the right kind of rude: efficient, demanding, and specific, with an expectation of excel-
lence. They were firm but respectful. And then there were
the other types: the ones who clicked their fingers or shouted,
pushed and complained, just to be heard. The first type of rudeness was born of confidence. It came from people who, no matter how wealthy they actually were, felt like they deserved to
be in this expensive, pretentious shop. The second type came
from the exact opposite. The ones who clicked their fingers and
talked down to the staff were the ones who felt like they needed
to prove to everyone that they belonged there. The ones who
didn't have the confidence to be calm and desperately needed
the people serving them to believe that they were important.
It didn't seem to matter that these people were dropping $370
on a children's party dress or $245 on a pair of flip-flops. They
needed us, the $11-an-hour staff, to be impressed.

I understand why these people were intimidated. The first
time my mother took me to Harvey Nichols (another, much

cooler department store with even fancier stock), I walked through the handbag hall, scared to even breathe next to the McQueen and Chanel. All the beautiful women with huge hair and red lipstick were terrifying, and I was convinced they were staring at me, assessing my outfit, concluding that I didn't belong. My mother gave short shrift to this. "You've got just as much right to be here as anyone else," she told me. "Don't be silly. It's just a shop."

Years on, I still occasionally have to tell myself, "It's just a shop," "It's just a bar," "It's just a party." I've added my own little mantra now, which goes something like, "They are at work, this is their job, they definitely don't care about you, they just want their shifts to be over so they can go home." Sometimes, especially if you're an anxious person, it can feel like everyone is interested in your behavior. Please believe me when I say that absolutely no one cares about your conduct as much as you do. No one is still thinking about that stupid thing you said last week or the way that you opened that door.

Say please, say thank you, tip generously, ask for what you want, complain firmly but politely if you don't get it, say yes if you mean yes and no if you mean no, and then move on. Technically, it is that simple. The only other tiny step is unlearning everything else about rudeness that you've ever known.

Hair

If you are a woman who cares about her hair, the hairdresser is a sort of safe space. You arrive feeling a bit ragged, and as long as things go right, you can leave feeling like a new woman—utterly transformed. The magic of the hairdresser isn't really magic at all. For lots of women it's the only time when they sit quietly and read a book or play with their phone without being interrupted by a child, a partner, a work crisis, or some other unavoidable irritation. Combine the magic of a couple of hours of selfish downtime with the transformative power of a really good blow-dry, and you can see why lots of us look forward to having our hair cut as if it's a demi-religious experience. Which is why it's a big deal when a haircut goes wrong.

When we talk about women's lives, we often do so in terms of moments, rites of passage, and watersheds: your first kiss, your first relationship, the first time you have sex. Those are all important. But I strongly maintain that there is another, more significant first: the first time that a woman gets a bad haircut.

My first bad haircut took place when I was fourteen. I was a little chubby, carrying a very unattractive sunburn on my nose, and generally convinced that I was hideous, as most of us are at that age. Previously I'd always had great haircuts that had left me feeling prettier, happier, and more like myself. On this occasion, things were different. I said I wanted an inch off, but the hairdresser insisted I needed far more than that. Intimidated, I agreed meekly and then felt that familiar sick feeling when the blow dryer came out and my previously middle-back-length hair barely brushed my shoulders.

We all know that if a haircut is bad, you're supposed to politely explain that you're not happy. Of course, I was fourteen and terrified, so this didn't occur to me. I paid and then cried all the way home, whereupon my mom gave me a big hug and welcomed me to adulthood. Crying after a trip to the hairdresser was, she told me, part of being a woman. Who among us hasn't said, "I love it, thank you," to a hairdresser while gulping back the tears and then ducked into a café bathroom to have a quiet sob in mourning for the hair that we've lost?

As a white woman with straight hair, I've had some hair disasters, but they're nothing compared to the experiences of some of the women of color I've spoken to, who have had their hair butchered by people who didn't know how to cut curly or textured hair. Maya, a twenty-nine-year-old writer from London, told me: "I've only met three hairdressers in my entire life who know how to cut curly hair properly. Every other one I've been to does a terrible job, and I say thank you and pay the bill.

"At the end of the haircut the hairdresser always offers to blow-dry my curly hair straight, and I always say yes, even though I'd rather they did it curly. A couple of years ago a hairdresser used such high heat trying to get it straight that she burned the top of my head. All the skin peeled off, giving me super dandruff for a month. But obviously I still paid her and said I loved it."

In the first season of *America's Next Top Model*—every teenage girl's '00s pleasure—a woman named Ebony Haith was told she was going to have her head shaved for her "makeover." The white hairdressers on the show had no idea how to handle Ebony's textured hair. The clip is agonizing to watch; the hairdressers laugh at their own inability while they make a complete mess of this woman's hair. Ebony herself, usually outspoken and confident, sits silently and seethes while they work, unable to find her voice to complain until after they've butchered her hair.

I've had four or five bad hair experiences since that first one, and only recently have I found my voice. Last year, a colorist mixed up two tubes and ended up highlighting my light blond hair a dark brownish orange. I knew it had gone wrong, she knew it had gone wrong, everyone was on the same page. There was a time when I would have meekly accepted the terrible color and paid to have it fixed. But, newly emboldened by the superpower of rudeness, I stood firm. I called the company I had booked the treatment through and asked for a refund, which I got. Then I returned to the salon, as they had offered to fix the color, and sat in the chair for eight hours while they made it marginally better. Then, rather than telling them I was delighted and smiling, I took a big deep breath and told them that it wasn't perfect, I wasn't happy, but I appreciated that they had tried to improve the situation. I've honestly never felt braver.

What you do after a bad haircut is a matter of taste—and depends on the laws where you live. In the UK you're not obliged to pay for a bad haircut, under the Consumer Rights Act. In the US the lines are a little more blurry, similar to whether you have to pay the bill if you've been served terrible food. I'm mostly inclined to pay, complain, ask for a different, more senior stylist at the salon to correct it, and, if they don't get it right, ask for a refund. But it's entirely up to you, and if you don't trust anyone at the salon, or you feel that they're unhygienic or not safely working with the chemicals, trust your instinct and get the hell out.

A bad haircut can easily be brushed off (ha ha) as a first-world problem. Beauty is vapid and pointless, right? It's only hair. But I will forever stand by my opinion that the hairdresser is where we as women can learn to rid ourselves of the fear of being rude.

I've caught myself—many times—saying that the water temperature for the shampoo is absolutely fine when it's too hot or too cold. What have I achieved by doing this? The person washing my hair doesn't care. It's not a huge imposition to change the temperature of the water. They are asking because they want to get it right. And yet time and time again we put our own comfort below the convenience of a stranger who is being paid to provide a service, at absolutely no benefit to that stranger.

Is this a tiny problem in the grand scheme of things? Of course. But it's also a big fat fucking metaphor for the way that we as women put our own wants, needs, and comfort right at the bottom of the pile.

Hair is not life or death. But that's why it's the perfect place to practice complaining. I can't help thinking that if someone had taught me to say, at age fourteen, "Actually, this wasn't really what I asked for and I'm disappointed with how it has turned out," I might not have spent the next decade and a bit trying to work out how to shake a pathological fear of seeming rude.

Restaurants

The reality of eating at restaurants means that sometimes, the food or service will fall short of your expectations. Sometimes the food will be a little cold, under- or overseasoned, or just not quite right. And for people who are fluent in the language of complaints, that's not a big deal. But of course for every one of us who can happily say, "I asked for my steak rare and this is well-done—I'd like another," there are those of us who will chew our way through a beef bourguignon despite being a committed vegetarian, purely to avoid being rude.

Before I was a writer, I worked as a nanny. One afternoon I took my charge to McDonald's (I didn't say I was a very good nanny), where she had a Happy Meal. The meal was supposed to come with a specific toy but hers came with another. She opened it and was enormously disappointed. "I wanted the one on the poster," she told me. And to be fair, when you're seven, that's quite a big deal. "Can you ask?" she asked me.

Sensing that this was a teachable moment (and why be a nanny if not to create the feminists of the future?), I said no, and instead offered to go the counter with her so that she could ask for the correct toy. She was nervous and could barely meet his eye but politely told the man behind the cash register that she would like the toy advertised if there was one available, and he gave it to her. He even let her keep both. And in that moment, I swear she grew three inches. I didn't impart much wisdom on her during my tenure, other than that Taylor Swift is a queen, no matter what anyone says, but the singular gift I did give was the ability to make a polite complaint. After that, whenever we went out to eat, she would inspect the hot chocolate, cupcake, or smoothie we'd bought, and on the rare occasion that something wasn't as advertised, she would quietly ask me, "Can I complain?"

Of course, there were times—like when she told me that her teatime sausages weren't hot enough—that I regretted imparting my lesson enormously. But, in the end, it was the most useful thing I did as her nanny. I taught her, before she had fully absorbed the message that women are not supposed to demand, or even ask for, things, that she had every right to make a polite complaint. Something that so many of us still struggle to do as adults.

Recently, I went to lunch with my mom, who happens to be an amazing cook and pretty expert in all things food. She ordered a piece of fish called a ray wing, and a little while later a plate of something completely different arrived. After a little bit of dithering, she called the waitress over and said: "I'm so sorry, but I don't think this is ray wing." The waitress assured her that it was ray wing and went on her way. My mother, who has cooked pretty much every piece of fish under the sun, silently fumed. She knew, without any shadow of a doubt, that she was right. And yet she didn't want to say anything, so she ate the mystery fish in silence.

At the end of the meal when the waitress came back, we repeated the question: are you sure that was ray wing? Of course, the answer was that it was indeed not ray wing and that the plates had been mixed up on the way out of the kitchen.

First-world problem? Of course. I doubt it was even the biggest catastrophe that happened in that restaurant that day, but it's a classic example of a woman ignoring her instincts for fear of making a fuss. Doing it once over lunch isn't a big deal, but it is a big deal if it becomes, as is the case for so many of us, a lifelong habit of accepting the mediocre while paying for better.

Many of the people who took the *Rude* survey said that they hate complaining in restaurants because it feels like they're taking out their frustration on their waiter or waitress, who is usually totally blameless and often very badly paid.

This raises an interesting dilemma. If you go out to eat and the service is slow, the food is cold, and the experience is generally underwhelming, it's not right that you should still end up paying full price, or that you should have to eat food that you don't enjoy. For many of us, eating out is a treat and something that we look forward to. It's not wrong to expect a certain level of care and quality. It's very noble to put up with bad food to spare the waiter, but it's also the same old problem—putting the needs of a stranger above your own for fear of seeming rude.

Lots of people who work in the food service industry are young, underpaid, and not having the most fun day. So, it can feel imperious, bordering on shameful, to summon said person to your table and tell them that the steak they brought over (which happens to cost more than their hourly wage) wasn't quite right. No one wants to be the bitch at table fourteen who snarls "Let me speak to your manager" to the teenage waitress who is only on her second-ever shift.

It's okay to speak to your server, though, without blaming

said server. Be polite and be clear that you know it isn't the underpaid waiter's fault. When they ask you how the food is, it is okay to be honest without blaming them for the chef's mistake. And, as long as the service was fine, your tip should reflect that.

Sometimes, though, you will encounter less-than-satisfactory service. A few years ago, I spent the weekend in Cornwall with my husband and another couple. At dinner we ordered a bottle of red wine and a bottle of white wine, and I was asked to try the white. I tried it, and lo and behold, it was fizzy. It was not supposed to be fizzy. I told the waiter that the bottle was corked and that we'd like a different one—something I'd never done before in my life. To my surprise he shook his head. "It's supposed to be like that," he told me.

It wasn't supposed to be like that. I've drunk more wine in my life than I care to (and can) remember, and I know what should and shouldn't be fizzy. "I don't think it is," I told him. "We'd really prefer another bottle."

"I can get you another bottle," he said, "but it will taste the exact same."

At this point I started to lose my temper, and instead of being a mature adult and saying "Yes, we'd prefer that," I decided to announce that I was a professional wine taster and that the wine was off. In case it isn't clear, I am not a professional wine taster. My wine drinking is strictly recreational.

The waiter, who couldn't have been more than twenty, looked a little surprised and duly brought another bottle. To my enormous relief, the second bottle was not fizzy, and we got on with the evening.

I was paying for that bottle of wine, and I'd been elected to try it. Those two factors should have been enough on their own to justify my request for a different, non-fizzy bottle of wine. There was absolutely no reason that I needed to claim to be a professional wine taster. The point of this story is to illustrate that it's easy to lack the courage of your convictions when you complain, and a robust waiter who tells you that you're wrong might well be convincing, but the old adage is correct: the customer is always right.

You don't need to be a professional wine taster to know if a bottle of wine is off, and you don't need to be an expert in Michelin-starred food to tell if a bowl of soup is too cold. You're paying for it. If you don't think it's right, then say so.

How to Complain

The key to complaining is to do it in a polite, measured, and respectful way, to ask the waitstaff for a quiet word and explain (ideally with a smile, and never with a raised voice) what the problem is and how you'd like it to be resolved.

"As a waiter, I never resented customers for complaining," said Liza, twenty-six. "They were generally right. I'm not dumb; I worked in and out of the kitchen and I could tell that our food wasn't always great. Honestly, as long as the customer was polite to me, I never felt any kind of animosity toward them about a food complaint. After all, it's not like I cooked it myself.

"I never feel annoyed if someone politely requests a change to their meal either," says Liza. "Sometimes it's annoying to have to go back to the kitchen because our chefs might shout at us, but that's not the customer's fault.

"Also, it makes life a lot easier if they say what they want. Your options are usually either a replacement for the food, a different dish from the menu, or to just have it taken off the bill. As long as you haven't eaten the whole thing, then everywhere I've worked has been happy to do any of those things, but it's quicker and easier if you explain from the outset which one you'd like it to be."

Complaining doesn't mean that you subsequently skip leaving a tip. In most restaurants the tip is for the waitstaff, not the chef, so if it's the food that you're complaining about, skipping the tip just means that the server who dealt with your complaint has been penalized, which is not fair. It's more appropriate to complain about the food but still leave a full tip.

If the service has been really terrible, then you might consider skipping the tip, but again, it depends on whether the restaurant is understaffed and the servers are doing their best, or if your server has truly been rude and acted like it was an imposition to take your order. If it's the former, consider being the bigger person and leaving a tip. If it's the latter, it's up to you.

When I go to a restaurant or hotel that is clearly understaffed, I will often email the management afterward to say that I had a great time and the staff were doing their best, but that they were clearly shorthanded and that they should consider hiring some extra team members. I'm sure that often these emails are ignored, but occasionally I get a reply saying that they've hired more people. Even if it achieves nothing, it means I've taken an active step to let the establishment know that they're not treating their staff fairly, and sadly a business is often more likely to listen to a customer than to a team member.

Complaining has changed a lot since the invention of the Internet. Whereas once upon a time we were obliged to tell people to their faces that their food was shit or their hotel was uncomfortable, now we can smile at the people in real life and send a snarky tweet. I'm not sure it's really brought out the best in anyone. Making a complaint in person allows you to explain to them directly why you're upset.

If you look at the tweets sent to rail companies, hotel companies, supermarkets, and restaurants, you'll see streams of abuse. People who are probably perfectly mild mannered in real life turn into complete monsters when they complain online, saying things like "I am disgusted" about a slightly late train or "You deserve to lose your jobs" over stale sandwiches. It's almost like years of not complaining in real life has created a social media pressure cooker where complaints are distilled to their strongest, angriest possible form.

This is the wrong kind of rude. If you can't stand by your rudeness in person, then there is probably something off about it. We're in the business of condoning the kind of rude that calmly asserts consumer rights and requests a timely replacement, not the kind of rude created by social media, which tells the person working in customer service to go fuck herself because the jar of salsa you've purchased is two days past its sell-by date.

During a train journey between Edinburgh and London,

my seat reservation was canceled. At first, I entered into a long fight with a social media staff member for Virgin Trains, painstakingly detailing every aspect of my subpar journey. But there was nothing he could do from a hundred miles away. In the end, I decided to take my frustration offline and dragged my bag and my husband to the first-class compartment, sat down, and, when asked whether I had a first-class ticket, explained what had happened and asked whether the ticket collector was really going to make me sit in the luggage rack for another six hours. To my relief, he did not.

It didn't matter how many furious tweets I sent from my Twitter account, nor did it matter that I had eighteen thousand followers and a blue "verified" check mark; the only way I was getting a seat was by making a polite face-to-face complaint. Complaining properly is assertive and respectable. Slinging abuse at strangers on the Internet—no matter how angry you are—is not the right kind of rude.

THE RIGHT KIND OF
Rude as a Consumer

▶ Do not click at waitstaff. Do not sleep with people who click at waitstaff. Do not be friends with people who click at waitstaff.

▶ There is nothing wrong with making a complaint as long as it is done politely.

▶ Complaining in person will usually get you a quicker result than making a complaint online.

▶ When you complain, you should also state how you want the issue to be fixed, rather than making the staff member play a guessing game.

▶ When it comes to allergies, you should be as rude as you need to be. Is it really worth playing fast and loose with your health?

▶ Anyone who makes you feel like a bad person for making a polite complaint has their own issues to deal with.

▶ After you've complained, it's still better to leave a tip, unless the waiter has been actively rude to you. If you're nervous about complaining, remember that you are still going to tip.

▶ Complaining can be done with a smile and should never, ever be done with a raised voice. If you lose your temper, you lose the argument.

- Try to remember that the business you're buying a service from isn't doing you a favor, so complaining isn't being ungrateful.

ROSA PARKS

◀ ▶

Rosa Louise McCauley Parks (February 4, 1913–October 24, 2005) was an American activist in the civil rights movement. She is often described as "the first lady of civil rights."

Parks was born in Alabama and grew up just outside of Montgomery. In 1932 she married Raymond Parks, who was a member of the NAACP. A year later she went back to finish her high school education, after having dropped out at age eleven to take care of her mother and grandmother. Later, in 1943, she became the secretary for the Montgomery chapter of the NAACP, writing in her autobiography, "I was the only woman there, and they needed a secretary, and I was too timid to say no."

Parks's activism didn't start or end with the bus boycott. In 1944, before the boycott, in her capacity as secretary of the

Montgomery NAACP, she investigated the gang rape of Recy Taylor, a black woman from Abbeville, Alabama. She helped to organize the Committee for Equal Justice for Mrs. Recy Taylor, which the *Chicago Defender* later described as "the strongest campaign for equal justice to be seen in a decade."

Segregation in Alabama was brutal and entrenched in every aspect of public life. In 1900, Montgomery had passed a city ordinance to segregate bus passengers by race. Conductors were empowered to assign seats to achieve that goal. According to the actual legislation, no passenger was required to move or give up their seat and stand if the bus was crowded and no other seats were available, but, perhaps predictably, Montgomery bus drivers started requiring black riders to move for white riders when there were no seats left in the whites-only section.

After finishing work on the evening of Thursday, December 1, 1955, Parks boarded the Cleveland Avenue bus in downtown Montgomery. She paid her fare and sat in an empty seat in the first row of the so-called colored section toward the back of the bus.

The bus then reached a stop where several white passengers boarded. The driver noted that two or three white passengers were standing, as the front of the bus had filled to capacity, so he moved the "colored" section sign behind Parks and demanded that four black people give up their seats so that the white passengers could sit.

The three other people moved, but Parks remained seated. The driver then called the police to arrest Parks.

Describing the incident in her autobiography, Parks wrote:

"People always say that I didn't give up my seat because I was tired, but that isn't true. I was not tired physically, or no more tired than I usually was at the end of a working day. I was not old, although some people have an image of me as being old then. I was forty-two. No, the only tired I was, was tired of giving in."

After her arrest, Parks became an icon of the civil rights movement. But the fairy-tale version of her story often skips over a few major factors, such as the fact that due to economic sanctions used against activists, Parks lost her job at the department store where she worked. Or that her husband had to leave his job after his boss forbade him to discuss his wife or her legal case. Still, Parks continued her work, and by the time she died, at age ninety-two, she was one of the most famous activists in the world.

Here's the thing: of course, Parks's refusal to give up her seat wasn't rude—it was simply right. Unquestionably, undeniably, unarguably right. But in the eyes of the people around her—the people who believed that white people deserved better treatment and special privileges—she was being extremely rude. And sometimes that's the thing about being rude: you have to act with integrity and allow yourself to believe that your judgment is correct.

Most of us will never do anything as brave as Rosa Parks, and most of us won't make a fraction of the difference to the world that she did. But we can hold on to that same sense of what around us is fair or unfair and try to act accordingly.

7 | RUDE
at
Work

Most of us had an after-school or weekend job as a teenager. It's a rite of passage. My first job was working in a local village shop, and the experience turned out to be my first real taste of how badly wrong things can go if you're afraid to be rude.

My job was simple—I worked behind the register of my local shop, which sold everything from sweets to sponges, between two p.m. and five p.m. Saturdays. Everything went fine until my second shift, when my coworker told me that we were entitled to one free drink per shift—quite a generous offering when you're making $3.70 an hour. Following her lead, I drank a Diet Coke, and then, unsurprisingly, I needed to pee. But I didn't want to be rude.

Peeing, despite being something that literally all of us do, had wiggled its way into my brain as something to be ashamed of. Something not to talk about. Something rude. I didn't know where the bathroom was, and I was too embarrassed by the rudeness of the question to ask. So, I made my way through a very uncomfortable few hours and the second I finished I legged it toward home. Unfortunately, the twenty-minute walk was more than my bladder could handle, and so I found myself having a pee in a bush by the side of the road. Not a dignified or a comfortable experience, I can assure you.

You'd think that the indignity of peeing in a bush would have been enough to hammer the message home: better to be rude than to suffer. But of course, it wasn't. It took more than ten years for me to learn that when it comes to the workplace, being rude is sometimes necessary. Before I learned that lesson, though, I let a boss refer to me as "whatshername" or occasionally "whatshername with the tits," let people take credit for my ideas, held my tongue in meetings, stayed late for no money or advantage, allowed my clothing to be critiqued, never asked for more money or seniority—the list goes on and on. And I wasn't the only one who allowed myself to be fucked over at work—women all over the world have had similar experiences.

Name Games

After I finished college, I started a job as a receptionist at a PR company in central London. My job was to answer the phone, organize catering for meetings, clear up and set up meeting rooms, and look after the office schedule. What followed was six months of smiling politely while people in suits exited conference rooms and left behind chewing gum in their coffee cups, used tissues on the tables, banana skins on chairs, and cookie wrappers on the floor. Not once did it occur to me to ask the people whom I worked with day in and day out to throw their own used tissues in the trash.

In my tenure as a receptionist, I also let people call me Becky. Every single day. When your name has more than two syllables, people seem unable to resist shortening it. My name is Rebecca, or very occasionally Bex. I don't want people to call me Becky—I have nothing against the name Becky, but it isn't my name.

Correcting someone who gets your name wrong should be about the easiest thing a person can do. "Oh, it's not Charlie, it's Charles"—six words and you've avoided the problem. But when you've been raised to prioritize shielding other people from discomfort over your own feelings, it's hard to potentially make someone else uncomfortable by simply saying, "That's not my name."

"I worked in an office for six years," said Nathalie, a thirty-five-year-old architect from London. "When I was very junior someone called me Nattie, and it stuck. I was called Nattie every single day, didn't matter who was talking to me—even the intern who was fifteen years younger than me, everyone called me Nattie. To start with, I felt too junior to say anything, like it would be precocious or disrespectful. Then after a while, when I'd been promoted, I felt too insecure to say anything, like it would make people think I was up myself and flaunting my promotion if I asked to be called by my full name. Eventually I left, and when I started my new job, I swore that I wouldn't let them call me anything other than Nathalie.

"On my first day someone asked if I went by Nat and I took a deep breath and said, 'Not really, no.' They called me Nat anyway and I couldn't bring myself to be rude and say, 'No, really, it's Nathalie.' It was a new job at a new firm, and I needed people to like me. Telling my coworker to use my full name felt like a rude thing to do, so I didn't. I've been there three years and people still call me Nat."

No doubt some would argue that being called by a diminutive that you didn't choose is no big deal. But it's called a diminutive for a reason—it literally diminishes your name. Makes it smaller. In a world where women struggle to achieve equal pay, something as simple as being called by the unshortened, more adult, and more assertive version of your name can make a difference.

Who are you more nervous to go into a meeting with, Rosie or Rosemary? Angelica or Jelly? Suzanna or Suze? Shortened nicknames are often what parents use to make their children's names sound more fitting for a baby. It might seem like a friendly gesture, but using a nickname for someone without their consent undermines them.

Apologies

By now, you will likely be totally unsurprised to read that women apologize more than men. Studies have shown this time and time again. According to a study published in *Psychological Science* in 2010, the reason for this is that "women have a lower threshold for what constitutes offensive behavior" and therefore are more likely to see a need to say sorry. You can say that again.

At the time of writing, it's two forty-five in the afternoon and I have already apologized for opening the door to my apartment building while someone was standing quite near it, for trying to get on a tube, wanting a lid for my coffee, and the fact that someone else on my team hadn't done a piece of work they were supposed to do. And that's me trying not to apologize too much.

Introducing the power of rude into your work life is easier said than done. Any noticeable change in your behavior is likely to confuse those around you. Banning the word "sorry" from your life is a great aim, but trust me, it's nearly impossible to actually do. However, what you *can* start doing straightaway is to reframe the way in which you apologize.

Saying you're sorry when you've actually done something wrong is great; it's a sign of strength to be able to acknowledge your own failings. However, there is a tendency for women to use "sorry" as a catchall, often when what they really mean is "thank you." If you can swap out those sorrys, you can assert yourself as a more competent person. Rather than saying, "I'm sorry for keeping you waiting," try "Thank you so much for your patience." Instead of "I'm sorry for not understanding," go with "Thank you for taking the time to explain." In doing so you're still acknowledging the favor done for you by the other person, but not by suggesting that you yourself are in the wrong. The person you thank feels that their efforts have been seen, but you haven't admitted any unnecessary fault.

Emails

Emails are a great place to observe just how scared many of us are to be rude. Most of us are probably guilty of filling our emails with self-deprecating language. The worst offenders are qualifying words like "just" and "quick," and statements such as "I'm no expert" and "Is there any chance?"

In an article published on LinkedIn, former Google employee Ellen Petry Leanse described an informal experiment that she led after she noticed that the women she worked with were constantly using the word "just" as a qualifier about their work ("I just wanted to ask," "I'm just going to edit that document," "I'm just wondering"). Leanse writes:

> In a room full of young entrepreneurs, a nice even mix of men and women, I asked two people—a guy and a girl—to each spend three minutes speaking about their startups. I asked them to leave the room to prepare, and while they were gone, I asked the audience to secretly tally the number of times they each said the word "Just." Sarah went first. Pens moved pretty briskly in

the audience's hands. Some tallied five, some six. When Paul spoke, the pen moved . . . once. Even the speakers were blown away when we revealed that count.

A 2006 study by Carol Waleski titled "Gender and the Use of Exclamation Points in Computer Mediated Communication," originally published in the *Journal of Computer-Mediated Communication*, found that women were more likely than men to use exclamation points as a softener in their email communication. Why? Because it makes you sound perky and enthusiastic rather than direct and confrontational. "Thanks for this!" reads as lighter and less serious than "Thanks for this." Women, the research concludes, are considerably more worried about how their written communication comes across. As one viral tweet said, "Behind every great woman are four other women who proofread her email for her real quick when they had a second."

In 2017 a man named Martin Snieder accidentally used his female coworker's email signature and noticed an immediate difference in the way he was treated by his correspondents. Out of interest, he continued doing so for the rest of the week and was shocked by the experience, writing on Twitter, "I was in hell. Everything I asked or suggested was questioned. Clients I could [usually handle] in my sleep were condescending. One asked if I was single."

In response to this discrepancy between how men and women email, plug-ins have been developed that highlight or underline every time you use qualifying words such as "just," "quick," "sorry," and "I think." Unfortunately, installing a plug-in so that your emails read as more confident and masculine (ruder, if you will) is not a catchall. In 2017, journalist Amelia Tait wrote an article for the *New Statesman* that detailed numerous case studies of women who email "like men" being regarded as aggressive or cold when they dropped the nice-lady language. She wrote: "Can women win? Without exclamations, they might seem rude—with them, they may seem unprofessional."

Of course, you shouldn't have to worry about any of this. It should be entirely possible for you to show up at work, do your job, and go home without anyone judging you based on the tone of your email or how smiley you are in the elevator. Sadly, that isn't the case. The world of work is not always kind to women—especially not rude women. In fact, there is an entire section of language devoted to smacking them back into their place—words that are only ever used to describe women who eschew hyperfeminine politeness.

- ballbreaker
- bitchy
- bridezilla
- catty
- diva
- feisty
- gutsy
- high-maintenance
- hormonal

- hysterical
- pushy
- shrill
- stroppy

With an entire lexicon of loaded language designed to shame women who are anything less than cheery at all times, is it really any wonder that we email with chirpy exclamation marks and end our missives by claiming that we "really hope that you're well"?

The vicious cycle goes on. We email like Office Barbie for fear of being seen as rude, and so it becomes expected that we will do so. Women who skip the smiley-face emojis and don't "hope that you're enjoying this lovely weather!" are written off as overly cold.

There is no easy solution and no magic wand to change the way that women are perceived in the workplace, or indeed in the world. Using the power of rude does sometimes mean that you are going to be perceived as cold or as a "ballbreaker," frustrating as that might be.

Hepeating

If you work in an office, then you may well be familiar with the sin of "hepeating," if not the term itself. The word was coined in 2017 and popularized by Professor Nicole Gugliucci, who explained the definition as: "When a woman suggests an idea and it's ignored, but then a guy repeats it, and everyone loves it."

149

Classic signs of hepeating are when men start sentences with "Just coming off the back of what [your name] said" or "To build on what [your name] said."

It's possible to dismiss hepeating as just another minor workplace irritation, but the problem is that hepeating can actually erode your career progress if the rest of the meeting attendees remember the last person to make a point (the hepeater) rather than the person who originally had the idea (you).

"I had a guy in my seminar group at university," says Clara, twenty-nine, "who would never read the book. Fair enough, that was his choice. But instead of just sitting quietly and letting us discuss the book, he would hepeat whatever we said. And the tutor just lapped it up, thinking this bloke was some kind of genius, when actually he was just taking the best part of what we said and slightly rephrasing it. Admittedly a lot of the problem was this tutor, who for some reason chose to ignore his copycat behavior, but this guy got top marks, was always paired with the best people in the class for group work, and generally coasted through without doing any work.

"Toward the end of the module I got really sick of it, so whenever he hepeated me I would just look him straight in the eye and repeat what I had said again. We'd go back and forward until the tutor stopped us. He stopped ripping my points off and I felt like on some level I had won."

Tackling hepeating at work is harder than doing it in a university environment, because at work, we're all supposed to act like functional adults. Occasional instances of hepeating might have to be ignored, but if you've got a regular hepeater, there's nothing wrong with an icy smile and a simple "Yes, which is what I was saying."

In 2017, CNBC asked Harvard public policy professor and behavioral economist Iris Bohnet, the author of *What Works: Gender Equality by Design*, what women should do if they are being hepeated. Bohnet suggested that the best way to combat hepeating at work is to invest in a kind of micro-sponsorship, which means enlisting a few coworkers to advocate for you when you've been wronged.

Bohnet explains: "Become vigilant about attributing comments to the people who made them first. Everyone, men and women, can become a micro-sponsor." Ultimately, Bohnet advocates for a system in which you have other people advocate on your behalf, and presumably you advocate for others too. So rather than someone else having to say, "Actually, I was talking," or "You just ripped off my idea," you say, "I think [colleague's name] was talking," or "Yes, I think that's what [colleague's name] was saying before." By interceding for others, you are not perceived to be self-promoting (though there's nothing actually wrong with being self-promoting, of course) and hopefully, you build a network of other people who will provide you the same service in return.

Should we need to go to these lengths to stop men from ripping off our ideas and presenting them as their own? Of course we shouldn't. But the idea here is to harness the power of rude to make your life easier, which unfortunately means dealing in facts, rather than ideals.

Salary

There is a misconception that women "aren't good" at asking for raises, and that myth is often pointed to as a major cause of the gender pay gap. The truth, however, is that women do ask for pay raises, but their methods are often unsuccessful. We'll cover the agony of rudeness and money more fully later on in the book, but I would be remiss if I talked about office-based rudeness without looking at the subject of raises.

For women who are afraid of being perceived as rude, asking for a raise is, admittedly, about as painful as it gets. You're expected to approach someone who has given you a job, tolerated your work, and paid you a salary and then announce that said salary isn't good enough. Asking for a raise feels spoiled, entitled, and ungrateful. Of course, it isn't any of those things, and if you don't ask for at least a small raise a year, then with inflation you can end up earning less than you did when you started at the company. But rudephobia is not bound by logic; it's born of a visceral nausea that arises whenever we approach doing something that might make people think we are rude.

A couple of years ago, I was working at a newspaper. I'd been there for a few years, had plenty of experience, and knew what I was doing. I was good at my job and I was happy with the way things were going—until I realized that I was being paid less than most of my colleagues, and that my daily rate was almost half what the National Union of Journalists, the journalists' trade union in the UK, recommended a journalist should be paid. So, after two weeks of worrying,

I requested permission from my manager to ask for a raise, and when that permission came I then sent an email to my big boss saying:

> *Dear [REDACTED], I'm so sorry to ask, but I was wondering if there was any chance that we might be able to discuss my day rate? I feel that I'm a valuable member of the team, my traffic is strong and I have been part of the organization for almost two years. I completely understand if not, but I would be keen to discuss it with you.*

Not exactly a persuasive argument, looking back, although, thanks to a kindly boss rather than my own moxie, I did get a small raise. It was still considerably less than the union-recommended day rate, but I was so shocked at my own boldness that it didn't occur to me for a second that I might attempt to negotiate.

Sometimes, though, women are punished for asking for a raise. Sara Laschever, coauthor of the book *Women Don't Ask*, says women who are assertive regarding issues like salary are often perceived as aggressive and suffer the consequences of that perception.

> They tend to get rebuffed, and socially ostracized. Other women see this and realize it looks scary and risky to behave like them. Far better, they think, to sit tight and wait to be offered whatever it is—a promotion, pay rise, good project—rather than ask for it.

Millie, twenty-seven, told me about her own experience, which is in line with what Laschever laid out above:

> I worked as an unpaid intern for several months after I graduated from art school. Eventually I was told that I was going to be offered a paid role and I was over the moon. Then I looked at the offer: it was less than minimum wage, with almost no holiday and no benefits. So I spent a whole day psyching myself up and then went to ask to renegotiate. My boss told me that he was hurt beyond belief that I could be so unkind to him. He told me that he was paying me out of his business and by asking for more I had insulted him. I couldn't live on what he was offering, so I had to leave. For years afterwards I was scared of asking for a raise because I thought it would mean that my boss started crying and telling me how rude and ungrateful I was.

Something of a catch-22, right? We don't ask for raises, so the pay gap is our own fault, but when we do ask for them, we're arrogant bitches who need to be reminded of our place. Or we're spoiled and ungrateful brats who don't really care about the work. You'd be forgiven for looking at that equation and deciding that there is no good answer.

But there is an answer, and you can probably guess what it is: rudeness. Most of us are taught that money is the ultimate taboo topic, but it shouldn't be. Push aside your discomfort (and the discomfort of your colleagues) and ask your coworkers what they make. That way, when you go in and ask for a raise, you can have evidence to back up your argument.

Employers hate when their employees have transparent conversations about money with one another—for good reason. A workforce of people who have ongoing discussions about salary is far more likely to ask for raises and get them. And for as long as women have to live with the sexist and unfair perception that asking for a raise means they don't love their job enough, the best way forward is to use the old-fashioned "I am Spartacus" rule. If everyone is asking for pay reviews, no one woman can be sacrificed on the altar of "she doesn't really seem to love her job."

Bossy

"Bossy" is a word that is almost never applied to men. Instead, it is usually used to describe little girls who like to organize or exhibit leadership skills. It's a way of framing those skills in a negative light. While some progress has been made, many young girls are still taught that they shouldn't exhibit traits typical of a boss. And those girls often grow up to be women who feel uncomfortable being in charge.

There are plenty of good reasons to fear being the boss. Shelley Zalis, CEO of the Female Quotient, wrote for *Forbes*:

> "An analysis of news coverage of CEOs by the Rockefeller Foundation found not only that the media covered the personal lives of female CEOs more frequently

than male CEOs, but that 80% of news stories pegged the blame for failed company turnarounds to CEOs when they were women, compared to just 31% when they were men."

But beyond the glass cliff (the expression used to describe when a woman is brought into a failing company to improve the diversity optics and is then blamed for being unable to save an unsalvageable business), female CEOs sometimes seem to exhibit a sense of discomfort at being the boss, often as a result of internalized misogyny. There will always be a tiny part of me that hears the word "boss" and sees Don Draper drinking a glass of Scotch in a glass corner office. And while neither you nor I need to feel guilty about that tendency, it rears its ugly head when we are offered leadership roles. An easy way to start to reshape your perception of power is to look at who you are surrounding yourself with. I try to follow a decent number of women in business—rather than just beautiful women in yoga pants—on social media. I do this so that every day I am exposed to images of and stories from professional women. It's a small adjustment, but social media has a huge role in shaping our perception of the world, and it's an almost instant way to refocus your mind.

Guilt

Nola, thirty-one, works in finance. She's always been a high-flyer. She got a top degree, joined a competitive new-graduate training program, worked her way up, and now has a senior role at a bank where she is about a decade younger than everyone else at her level. After Nola had been working at the bank for a couple of years, the CEO requested that she apply to replace the person who had been managing her. Nola was queasy about doing it, citing her already strained work-life balance. But the CEO assured her that it wouldn't be that much more work because she would be able to delegate to her team.

When Nola was offered the job, we sat on my patio drinking wine and she told me that she felt guilty. "The other guy who applied is in his midforties," she told me. "He's got kids and a mortgage. He needs the money more than I do, and if he doesn't get promoted soon then he'll probably miss out."

Like any good girlfriend would, I told her that she had to take the role and that she deserved it, but she still turned it down at first. In response, the bosses offered her an added retainer bonus. The entire situation seemed perfect. More money, her own office, a bigger team. The dream. So, on the advice of all of her friends, Nola took the job.

Nola is a genius at her job. But the next time I saw her, she arrived two hours late to meet me for a drink and was clearly exhausted. It was nine p.m. and the earliest she had left work for weeks. When pressed, she told me that she was doing her own workload and then staying hours and hours after close to redo the work done by her team members or finish things that they hadn't had time to do. She was doing the work of her deputy—the man who had applied for her job—as well as all of her own, because she couldn't bring herself to confront the man she'd beaten out for the role. "It was so embarrassing for him that I got the job," she told me. "I didn't want to add to that by telling him off. He knows I won't say anything to him, so he just does whatever he wants."

This isn't a neat anecdote, because at the time of my writing this, Nola is still pulling eighty-hour weeks and sleeping five hours a night, and views her marathon training as "a rest." She claims that she's getting better at telling her team that they need to do their own work. But unfortunately, once you institute a certain workplace culture—especially one in which you pick up the slack for your colleagues—it's hard to undo it.

Orson Welles apparently used to hire someone especially so he could then fire him on the first day of a production, thus demonstrating that he was a tough guy who meant business. While that's obviously a bit on the extreme side, you can see where Orson was coming from. If Nola had walked into the job and stamped her authority all over the place, she wouldn't still be in a situation where she writes reports for people who should in theory be getting her coffee.

THE RIGHT KIND OF
Rude at Work

▶ Correct someone the day that they get your name wrong, not a week later.

▶ Keep written records of anything high stakes, so if anyone suggests that your tone was aggressive or harsh, you'll be able to demonstrate otherwise.

▶ Ask about pay grades, and encourage clarity surrounding how much everyone is earning. If you find out that you're being paid less, don't give a second thought to asking for a raise.

▶ Asking for more money might feel stressful and scary, but remember, unless you work for a very small business, a raise of $2,000 that would make a tangible difference to your life will make very little difference to the company's bottom line.

▶ Burnout is a real thing: if your company is working you too hard or setting unrealistic deadlines, you should say something.

▶ Calling people out for sexist behavior doesn't have to make you a killjoy. You can do it with a smile. Pro tip—if someone is telling sexist jokes in your office, pretend you don't get the joke and ask them to explain it. Continue to not understand until they've dug themselves into a nice big hole.

▸ Just because someone is senior to you, that does not give them the right to treat you with anything other than respect.

TAYLOR SWIFT

◀ ▶

In case you've been living under a rock, Taylor Swift is a multi-award-winning, stadium-filling, multiplatinum-selling singer-songwriter who, at age fourteen, convinced her parents to move from Pennsylvania to Nashville in order for her to focus on her career.

On one hand, the cookie-baking, cat-loving Taylor Alison Swift is as sweet as Ben & Jerry's Chocolate Fudge Brownie. She invites her fans over to her house to listen to her music. She loves homemade baked goods. She loves her cats and her mom. She grew up on an actual Christmas tree farm. And yet, more so than any other woman in the music industry, Taylor Swift embraces the power of rude when it comes to defending her rights as an artist and a creator.

In 2015, Apple Music decided that they would only pay

artists for streams by users who were outside of the free three-month trial period. Taylor Swift publicly told them that they couldn't use her music unless they paid for it, and as a result, Apple had to rethink their entire strategy and pay artists fairly.

In June 2019, Scott Borchetta, the owner of Taylor's record label, Big Machine Records, sold the company to Scooter Braun. Which was unfortunate for Taylor, because Scooter had publicly mocked her during the Kardashian-West saga of 2017. After the sale, all of the music that Taylor had recorded for Big Machine now effectively belonged to someone whom she hated. A bitter pill to swallow, given that these songs were a record of her life, her feelings, and her emotional development from child to adult. Even more bitter given that this was all a result of a contract she signed when she was fifteen. Many performers would have privately mourned the loss of their work and put a happy face on, afraid of angering the people they had previously worked with. Not Taylor.

When the sale was announced, Taylor released a statement that read:

I learned about Scooter Braun's purchase of my masters as it was announced to the world. All I could think about was the incessant, manipulative bullying I've received at his hands for years.

Like when Kim Kardashian orchestrated an illegally recorded snippet of a phone call to be leaked and then Scooter got his two clients together to bully me online about it. (See photo) Or when his client, Kanye

West, organized a revenge porn music video which strips my body naked. Now Scooter has stripped me of my life's work, that I wasn't given an opportunity to buy. Essentially, my musical legacy is about to lie in the hands of someone who tried to dismantle it.

This is my worst case scenario. This is what happens when you sign a deal at fifteen to someone for whom the term "loyalty" is clearly just a contractual concept. And when that man says, "Music has value," he means its value is beholden to men who had no part in creating it.

Unsurprisingly, the businessmen up top weren't pleased about Taylor taking the fight public. Five months later, Taylor made another public statement, saying that she had exhausted all avenues of negotiation with them privately and that Big Machine was trying to block her from performing a medley of songs *that she wrote* during the American Music Awards. She instructed her many millions of fans to let Scooter and Scott know how they felt about this situation and to pressure Scooter's clients not to stand for his behavior.

It was a move so ballsy that even I, the rude evangelist, took a sharp intake of breath when I read it. She was pulling no punches, putting the entire weight of her fame behind stopping these men from playing God with her work. And it worked. Big Machine allowed her to perform the work, and as of November 2020, she'll be free to record new versions of her older songs, which she'll own.

We're not all like Taylor. In fact, basically none of us are. We don't have millions of fans, sold-out stadium tours, and multiple houses. But women all over the world know what it feels like to watch someone else—usually a man—profit from our work. How often, when that happens, do you speak up, rather than simply allowing it to happen?

Of course, as this book acknowledges, women who transgress don't often get away with it. Swift has been smacked down time and time again, by the press, on social media, by other celebrities, for her refusal to remain silent. There are, predictably, people all over the Internet commenting that it was her own fault for signing the contract, that she should shut up and get over it, that she's making a fuss over nothing. But that's the thing. Whether it is singing about boys who cheated on her, writing lyrics about friends who screwed her over, or taking on multinational corporations who don't want to pay her, Taylor has never been willing to keep her mouth shut—something that we could all stand to emulate in our own lives. That's why her unflinching refusal to cave to Borchetta and Braun is so important.

As Taylor Swift demonstrates, you don't have to choose between being a nice person and being a rude person. She can bake gingerbread and send her fans gifts, but she can also shout down powerful men who want to prevent her from singing her own songs. She can be sexy and serious, hard and soft, beautiful and professional, rude and kind. And so can you.

8 | RUDE
About Money

Money and Friends

Talking about money in a professional setting is bad enough, but doing it with friends can sometimes be even worse. Just watch a group of people split a bill in a restaurant and you'll see. Even though everyone knows that paying for what you actually ate is fairer, splitting the bill evenly is very common. Doesn't matter if one of you had a side salad and a glass of tap water while someone else washed down the chateaubriand with a lovely 2011 Malbec. Possibly because if you're rich enough not to care, then you won't give it a second thought, and if you're the member of the group who is deciding whether to default on your water bill or say the words "Would anyone mind paying for what we had?" then you're probably lacking in the confidence to do so. There shouldn't be any shame in being the friend in the group who earns the least, but there often is.

Few words strike fear into my heart quite as much as "group birthday meal." I went to a birthday dinner recently at an incredibly expensive new restaurant in central London. I was feeling pretty broke after a spate of birthdays and wasn't really in the mood to attend. Neither was anyone else I knew who was going, but we slapped on smiles and turned up, having agreed between us that it wouldn't be more than about $50 a head if we ordered sharing plates and didn't eat too much.

We might have been right, if someone hadn't brought a girlfriend along. Said girlfriend—let's call her Jane—announced she wasn't hungry, so she didn't order anything, but, when the food arrived, she picked at everyone else's entrées and had four glasses of wine. At the end of the meal it was decided at her end of the table that she wouldn't pay because she "didn't eat." All of us who were already stressed about the bill gritted our teeth, ignored the added price of the four expensive glasses of wine, and took out our cards. Did we say anything? Of course not. We didn't want to be rude. Instead, we paid for this stranger's food and drink and seethed silently about it all night. The birthday girl felt guilty, we felt shortchanged, and it left a sour taste about the whole evening. If we'd been less afraid of being rude, we would politely have pointed out that she'd drunk a bottle of wine and asked her to pay. She probably wouldn't even have minded. The most frustrating part wasn't so much the money but the simmering resentment that we felt toward her for the rest of the evening.

Instead of letting our anger fester, we should have just said, "Does Jane want to put in some cash for her drinks?" If she'd then said that she couldn't afford to, we'd have at least known that was the reason she wasn't paying, rather than assuming she was just the wrong kind of rude and expecting us to pay for her. Generally speaking, the moment you admit to being hard up, the people who love you will feel sympathetic toward you and try to help you out or offer to socialize in a more affordable way. But if you don't bite the bullet and admit that you're trying to save money, the people around you might just assume that you're being tight.

Borrowing Money

Once, at college, my card was declined when I was trying to buy a six-pack of Diet Coke and some pita bread. I had a week until I was due to get any more cash into my account and I was panicked. Ashamed of myself, too proud to call my parents, and too afraid of seeming rude to ask my friends, I used a payday loan site to borrow $60, at nearly 6,000 percent APR. I was due to pay back around $105 a week later—a ridiculous amount, but manageable. Unfortunately, there was a glitch at their end and the payment wasn't taken, meaning that I was charged a $60 default fee. I then spent $50 on my phone bill trying to speak to the loan company to correct this. All in all, my refusal to swallow my pride and do the sensible (rude) thing of asking if a friend could spot me cost me $155.

Since then, I've borrowed money from and lent money to friends, following the rule that you should never lend more than you can afford to lose. There's a reason for the expression "Neither a borrower nor a lender be."

Sara, now twenty-eight, then twenty-four, lent her boyfriend $2,500 to help him get out of debt. She explains: "He didn't ask, to be fair. But he was struggling with his debt situation so I offered to pay it off and then he could pay me back slowly. He was enormously grateful and to start with he was making regular payments. But bit by bit they became later, less regular, and then when we broke up for unrelated reasons, they stopped.

"Years later, I found out that he had a really well-paying job, so I decided to get in touch with him. I spent two days crafting a really thoughtful email to send him, explaining that I wanted the money back but that I was willing to wait, take the payments slowly, whatever he needed. He didn't reply.

"In the end the whole conversation was bad for my mental health, so I decided to leave the money. But I'm still so angry with my past self for being so afraid to seem like a bitch by demanding that money back when we first broke up."

Caitlin, thirty-one, had a similar situation. She explains: "I covered a lot of bills and other costs when I moved into a shared house with two of my girlfriends. At first, I was too caught up in the fun of living together to chase for the money, and then it seemed too late, and kind of mean to ask. When I did eventually get the confidence to ask them, they ignored the message and I wasn't bold enough to ask again. They both still owe me a hundred fifty pounds each."

So lending money can go wrong, and demanding money back can be a terrifying thing to do, especially if you haven't yet embraced the idea of being rude. But, as awkward as it is, try to keep discussions of money (whether you're borrowing or lending) as straightforward as possible. Don't bully your friends when asking for repayment, but don't put the topic off until it is too late. These are your friends, after all. If you're close enough to someone to lend them money (or borrow from them), you should be close enough to have a straightforward conversation about said money.

Money and Relationships

Being honest about your finances is difficult with your friends, but it can be even harder in a relationship. At the start of a romance, the last thing you probably want to do is turn down something fun because you can't afford the ticket or come across as stingy by not offering to split the bill in an expensive restaurant. But if you don't get rude about money early on, then you make a rod for your own back.

When I first met my husband, I was an aspiring journalist/student/office temp. He is ten years my senior and was in a professional role with a good salary, so already there was an enormous gap in our finances. He was incredibly generous, but I was determined not to let him pay for everything, and rather than saying, "Actually, do you mind if we have a bottle of wine at home rather than three rounds of drinks at a pub?" I went further and further into my overdraft. When he was eventually laid off and had to start watching the pennies, I felt guilty about how relieved I felt. It was awful for him, but for me, the pressure was finally off.

Much of being in a relationship is about being honest about your wants, needs, and fears, and that hopefully will get easier as your relationship develops. But on the other hand, the longer you are with someone, the more tangled your finances get, and that's not necessarily a good thing. Joining your money with another person's might seem practical if you live together or you've got a lot of shared expenses, but it's important to be cautious about how you do that.

Claire, twenty-eight, found that combining finances was not a good idea. "About two years into my relationship with my then-boyfriend, we decided to merge an account and put our finances more together, seeing as we were moving in together.

"I'll be honest, I wasn't sure that I wanted to do it, but he said it made more sense, and when I talked about my concerns, he thought that I was rejecting him. I was scared to seem selfish or like I was being stingy, so I went ahead and did it. Unfortunately, it turned out that he had some major debt issues. He was working to pay it off, but lots of things were registered to our shared address and because we had a joint account it had a strong adverse effect on my credit rating.

"I've always been financially conservative to the point of being boring, so when I saw that my credit score had taken a massive hit, I assumed it was a mistake, but then I realized it was because of Chris, and I was horrified. Neither of us knew that there would be any issue with his credit rating affecting mine, and he didn't do it maliciously. But if I'm honest, I struggled to forgive him for it. I wanted to buy a house, something which has been delayed by this experience.

"In the end we broke up, and while I told him it had nothing to do with his debt and my credit rating, that isn't totally true. I was still too angry with him for pushing me into a joint account, and with myself for being too spineless to say no."

Mission Creep

Lately, stories of scammers and con artists have dominated the Internet. It is unlikely that you'll be a victim of a con any time soon, but the most common victims are women—especially women who aren't good at saying no.

A more common experience than being actively conned by someone is mission creep. Mission creep is when you end up paying for more and more of the costs of a relationship, until eventually you are basically supporting someone else financially. No one wants to be the girlfriend who says, "Why haven't you offered to buy groceries recently?" or "Why is it me who always picks up toilet paper?" but you can end up incurring a heavy financial penalty for being the more organized person who sets up the accounts to pay the bills or stops at the store on the way home from work. The only way to avoid this situation is to be open about your spending and your expectations and to name the beast when you feel that someone else is not pulling his weight in terms of the wallet.

It's fine to support another person by taking more of the financial load, if that's a conscious choice that you have made and one you feel able to handle. What you must not do is sleep-walk into being the sole provider of household essentials because you don't want to seem like a nag for asking your partner or roommate to do their part. In the end, anyone who is worth being in a relationship with will understand your financial barriers. And it might be the case that the other person just hasn't realized how often you pick up groceries or new sponges or lightbulbs. If this is the case in your situation—if your partner somehow seems to think that new toilet paper just magically appears every few weeks—you should speak up. Not only have you been spending more time on housework, but you've also been spending more money than they might even realize.

Anyone who makes you feel guilty for being blunt about money is not someone you should tie your finances to.

THE RIGHT KIND OF
Rude About Money

▶ It is always okay to tell someone, "I can't afford it."

▶ An invitation to an event is not a summons. If it's not in the budget, then you can explain that, or you can just turn down the invitation. Remember, "No" is a complete sentence.

▶ Before you combine your finances with someone, ask about their debt level and credit history. If they find this objectionable, then that tells you something—and probably not something good.

▶ Borrowing money from friends is a recipe for disaster, but sometimes it's unavoidable. Mitigate risks by writing down your agreement. You might feel silly at the time, but it'll come in handy if there's an argument.

▶ Don't stretch yourself to afford something that someone else wants.

▶ There's nothing wrong with debt—most of us have some. Refuse to feel ashamed about your debt, and talk about it honestly. The reason debt causes pain is because we allow ourselves to be ashamed of it.

▶ Trust your gut. If you think you're being ripped off, don't be afraid to say something.

ANNE LISTER

◄ ►

Anne Lister, born in England in 1791, was a diarist and businesswoman. She was also a (relatively) open lesbian. In 1826, following the death of her uncle James Lister, Anne inherited a property in West Yorkshire called Shibden Hall. In the 1800s, the idea of a woman running an estate, which entailed managing the finances and collecting rents from tenants, was almost unthinkable. And yet Anne did it—with great success. While Anne is perhaps most famous for her lesbianism and the four million words' worth of diaries she wrote, she was an impressive businesswoman who didn't let fears of societal standards or expectations stop her from doing battle with fellow industrialists.

According to Helena Whitbread, who decoded many of Anne's diaries, which were written in a complex code, "her entrepreneurial flair, her acquired knowledge, over the years, of mathematics, geology and engineering and her sharp negotiating skills with her male business rivals made her a formidable businesswoman in the newly-emerging world of industrialization, as is indicated in the following exchange with her defeated rival in the fight for selling coal in the area."

Anne wrote in her diary: "Mr Rawson said he was never beaten by ladies & I had beaten him. Said I gravely, 'It is the intellectual part of us that makes a bargain & that has no sex, or ought to have none.'"

Much is made of Anne's sexual adventures, which were, admittedly, impressive, varied, and staggeringly modern—she even had the equivalent of a marriage to another woman. There is no question that her commitment to living a sexually authentic life was brave in the extreme, especially as Anne received harassment and abuse for her same-sex relationships, unusual style of dress, and boldness in matters of business—a depressingly familiar concept even two hundred years later.

Anne Lister is the perfect example of just how much you can get away with if you suspend your fears of being rude. If a woman who lived more than two centuries ago was able to ignore naysayers and build a successful empire (much of which hinged on demanding money from men) without fear, then doesn't it follow that we should feel able to do the same?

Whether or not Lister was rude socially isn't clear, but I have no qualms in arguing that she was rude AF in general. Her diaries and biographies make clear that Lister did not give a fuck what anyone thought of her: she had loads of affairs, called a woman she considered sleeping with "new money," and must, unquestionably, have been pretty ballsy in order to keep control over her estate. Anne enjoyed a wide and varied sex life, a booming business, and a fearsome reputation, all before the invention of electricity.

She is a testament to just how much we can get done if we stop wasting time worrying what people think of us.

9 | **RUDE**
About
Health

During the time that I was writing this book, I had a miscarriage.

It started in Greece, when I was on vacation for my husband's birthday. I went to the bathroom and saw a few small spots of blood when I wiped. I'd never fully understood the expression "gripped with terror" before, but there I was, in a hotel room in Greece, feeling like the weight of the entire building was crashing around me.

We agreed there was nothing we could do. The Internet said that it was normal to have some bleeding in pregnancy (I was about eight weeks pregnant), so I lay down on the bed (as if gravity could save the pregnancy) and read *Crazy Rich Asians* until I couldn't keep my eyes open anymore. And the next morning the bleeding had stopped. Thank God, I thought.

A week later, I was back in London when the same thing happened. I think on some level I knew at that moment. My husband ordered an Uber and we went to our nearest emergency room, where upon arrival we stood in a line for twenty minutes to get to the reception area while I tried not to sob.

I try to avoid complaining about the National Health Service because I think it is the greatest thing about the UK, but in this instance, I was shocked by how cold, cavalier, and careless the staff were. I explained politely that I was pregnant, was bleeding, and needed to see someone ASAP. The receptionist remained stone-faced as she told us to go to the waiting area to await triage. After lots of waiting, I began to lose my mind. But my phobia of seeming rude really comes out when I'm at a UK hospital; it's a gift to have this kind of health care, and the doctors are overworked and underpaid. It has been drilled into me since I was a small child that you do not complain about the NHS, so I didn't complain. Instead, I lay down on the floor, again clinging to the idea that by lying down I could avoid gravity and keep the pregnancy. Logical? Of course not. But you're rarely logical in these moments.

Eventually, I was sent into triage, where I was told by a nurse that he wouldn't help me. "Either it's a miscarriage or it isn't," he said. "And we're not going to find out tonight." I got up, with as much dignity as someone who thinks she might be losing a pregnancy can possible have, and I looked him in the eye. "I suggest that perhaps you request some further sensitivity training from your line manager," I said. "Because your care this evening has been less than appropriate, and you've made a very difficult experience even harder."

I don't think I've ever used a frostier, more venom-filled voice and icier facial expression. And to this day, I sometimes worry that I did the wrong thing—he'd had a long day, probably, and English wasn't his first language, so he might well have missed a nuance in his words—but deep down, though I feel guilty for being ungrateful to an NHS staff member, I'm glad I said what was on my mind.

Had I not said anything, I would still be fuming toward him. What am I writing? I *am* still furious with him. He'd shrugged his shoulders over my miscarriage, like I'd asked him if he had seen my keys or whether he wanted salami on his pizza. The little speech I made probably hasn't changed anything, though I very much like to pretend that it did. I want to believe that next time a woman comes in with mascara tracks down her cheeks and an outfit she scrabbled together as she rushed to leave the house, he'll try to be a little kinder to her.

And even though I'm still angry at the rude nurse, I know that had I not said something, I would be even angrier now. I'm already carrying around the sadness of having had a miscarriage, so at least the weight of my anger is slightly diminished. I'm proud that I practiced what I preach. I was rude in a calm, moderate, practical way.

REBECCA REID

Lady Problems

There are some medical problems that only affect women. Quite a lot of them, actually. Funnily enough, these seem to be the ones that are most widely ignored, misdiagnosed, or brushed off as period pain.

In an episode of *Fleabag*, Kristin Scott Thomas gives an astonishing monologue about the nature of women and pain. She tells Phoebe Waller-Bridge: "The fucking menopause comes and it is the most wonderful fucking thing in the world! And, yes, your entire pelvic floor crumbles and you get fucking hot and no one cares, but then you're free. No longer a slave, no longer a machine, with parts. You're just a person in business.

"And that's the thing, isn't it? If men are in pain, there is something wrong, therefore they must be taken seriously. But there is a laundry list of lady reasons that a woman might be in pain, so if she is suffering you might as well fob her off with some paracetamol [acetaminophen] because the chances are that it's nothing. Or that it's something, but that the something is just part of being a woman."

Countless studies have shown that when it comes to pain, men and women are treated differently. One study by the Academy of Emergency Medicine, for example, found that women in the emergency room who report having acute pain are less likely to be given opioid painkillers than men. Another study from the University of Maryland found that women who go to the emergency room are less likely to be taken seriously than men.

A 2014 study from Sweden found that once they get to the

180

emergency room, women wait significantly longer to see a doctor and are less often classified as an urgent case.

This discrepancy can have lethal consequences. In May 2018, a twenty-two-year-old woman in France called emergency services saying her abdominal pain was so acute she felt she was "going to die." Instead of taking her seriously, the operator replied: "You'll definitely die one day, like everyone else." When the woman was taken to the hospital after a five-hour wait, she had a stroke and died of multiple organ failure.

It isn't our fault that women aren't taken as seriously as men are by doctors. But many of us take for granted that we'll be brushed off by health care professionals and thus, over time, become less confident in our own assertions about our bodies. It is common to read about women who have polycystic ovary syndrome or endometriosis—both of which often include menstrual cramps and irregular periods as symptoms—being told by a doctor that there is nothing wrong and continuing to live their lives with a chronic condition.

And women of color have it even worse than white women. In 2018, women of color took to Twitter en masse to share their stories of having their pain and medical issues ignored. "It took me blacking out at work, my mom threatening the doctor who thought I was a drug addict because I was screaming from being in pain before another doctor came and saw me. I was diagnosed with severe PCOS with a cyst the size of a grapefruit on my ovary and stage 4 endometriosis," tweeted Ashley E. Foster.

"Like Serena [Williams], I almost died of massive blood clots in my lungs and legs. The doctors initially said I just needed to lose weight. It wasn't until my blood pressure crashed to 60/20 that they finally accepted something was wrong. I was in the ICU 12 days," posted Helena Hamilton.

It's not just anecdotal evidence either. There have been many academic studies that demonstrate that women of color, most of all black women, are likely to be denied investigative medical treatment when they are ill and less likely to be provided with the pain relief that they require. A 2016 study published in the National Academy of Sciences found that "black Americans are systematically undertreated for pain relative to white Americans." Which might go some way to explaining why there is an average of a seven-year gap in life expectancy between black and white people living in the United States.

Doctors need to work to overcome their biases, without a doubt. But you also know your own body, and you know when something isn't right. So, if a doctor tries to dismiss your medical problem—especially if it's a female-specific one—then that's the moment to find your inner rude. There is nothing wrong with asking for further tests or a scan to figure out what is wrong with you. If you're incorrect and it is just period pain, then fine, but if not, you've saved yourself a lot of time and even more pain by insisting on finding out.

One doctor, who wanted to speak to me off the record, suggested that while none of this should be necessary, women should attend appointments with as much "evidence" as they can muster. "If you have an issue which may be related to reproductive issues, then using a period-tracking app like Clue and putting as much information into it as possible will be helpful.

Keeping a diary of any other symptoms, bringing a knowledge of your family's medical history—all of this will help you to be taken more seriously. You shouldn't need to, I know that. I struggle every day with the biases I see from my colleagues, toward women, toward specific racial groups. I wish it wasn't the case. But while we have to push for change, we also have to protect our patients and help them to get the best standard of care from a broken system."

Miscarriages

There are different types of miscarriages; some of them happen "naturally," and some need intervention. The one I had while writing this book was the latter. It's sometimes called a "missed" miscarriage because your body doesn't expel the pregnancy and continues to make pregnancy hormones. Due to the nature of my miscarriage, I had to have medication—two pills inserted at the neck of my vagina—to make my uterus contract and expel the pregnancy tissue. Unfortunately, this didn't totally work. It turns out that my body isn't very good at having a miscarriage, and I was left with some tissue at the top right-hand corner of my uterus, which made the surgery I would need to extract it more complicated. I asked the kindly doctor who explained this to me whether this meant that I had tissue in the worst possible location, and he responded by saying, "We don't like to use the word 'worst.'" I took his response as a yes.

I had to wait four weeks between finding out I had miscarried and having the surgery, with the pills taken in the middle. It was one of the worst periods of my life. As an added extra, I started having nightmares. Vivid, long dreams that objects—lengths of plastic tubing mostly—were falling out of my vagina covered in my blood. Or, even worse, I was giving birth to a tiny, perfectly lifelike baby doll. Suffice it to say, I wasn't having much fun. Several medical professionals—ones who actually seemed to take me seriously—told me that these dreams sounded like PTSD. I brushed off their comments because PTSD is for people who've been to war zones. That's the funny thing about a miscarriage: you're left to look after yourself, you go the bathroom and feel large chunks of tissue falling out of your vagina, and then you wash your hands and get on with it.

I went to a wedding the day that my miscarriage was in full force. I've never felt sicker or sadder, but I smiled and drank cocktails and put on a show. Halfway through the afternoon my underwear became unable to support the size of sanitary napkin required for my bleeding, so I asked my husband for his—he spent the rest of the day commando, while I wore his boxer briefs. In retrospect, it was complete madness not to spend the day at home, crying and bleeding in private, but I didn't make much of a fuss because I'd never known anyone else to make a fuss about a miscarriage, so it seemed like I was just supposed to get on with my life.

The rules surrounding miscarriage leave vary depending on where you live. In the UK, a doctor can recommend and sign off on a woman taking a leave of absence from work if she's recently suffered a miscarriage. But it's all at the doctor's discretion. If a woman loses a pregnancy after twenty-four weeks, though, she is entitled to bereavement leave.

In the US, the rules change from state to state and from employer to employer. Some employers offer paid bereavement leave, whereas others expect a woman to return to work the day after a miscarriage.

After my miscarriage, I was lucky—or as lucky as you can possibly be in that terrible situation. I'm a freelance writer with an extremely understanding editor who treated me like I was made of glass in the wake of my loss. He didn't raise an eyebrow when I said I wasn't able to come into work. Most women are not so lucky.

I can't imagine the pain of having to beg a doctor to sign off on bereavement leave after losing a much-wanted pregnancy, but that's what women have to do. And if the doctor says no, you just go back to work. Never mind if you're still bleeding, still seething with pregnancy hormones, still bursting into tears every time you see a targeted advertisement on Instagram for maternity wear. You get on with it.

I had intended to include a link to a petition for women to be given automatic miscarriage leave. But I couldn't find one, because at the time of writing, there wasn't one.

And I understand that. I've never felt less like being rude than I did after my miscarriage. I had no energy at all, so I definitely didn't have the energy to start a country-wide campaign to change the law. Being rude takes time. Effort. Fight. All of which had been knocked out of my body after my miscarriage. But, as is the case with so much of female health care, it's a vicious circle. We don't demand more because we're used to being treated like we don't deserve more, and because we don't demand it, we don't get it. And so, nothing changes.

Fat Shaming

When I was seven weeks pregnant, I went for my first maternity appointment. I was terrified: I'd put on seven pounds. I was so madly hungry all the time, and having given up smoking and drinking cold turkey, I felt like I could eat whatever I wanted. I'd heard horror story after horror story about women who'd been told off for too much weight gain during pregnancy, and after having spent much of my teenage years bingeing and purging, I was not in the mood for a relapse-triggering lecture about my weight. To my enormous delight, though, when I arrived at the clinic and was handed over to my midwife, I found that she was a very full-figured, very tall woman who presumably wasn't obsessed with weight. She certainly didn't say a cross word about mine.

I'm a US size 10–12, depending on how close to Christmas we are, so my personal experience of medicalized fat shaming is limited. I'm sure if I asked my GP whether I should lose some weight, she would say yes, as I am overweight. However, in all the time that I have spent in the hospital, which has been quite a lot recently, I've never had anyone comment on my weight or suggest that it requires management. Unfortunately, this is not the case for lots of plus-size women, especially women who are at the higher end of the weight spectrum. When you are not thin passing (an expression used to describe women like me who are not thin but are not fat in a noticeable way), having a doctor blame absolutely everything on your weight is a common experience.

Jess, twenty-four, lives in Oxfordshire. "I'm a size twenty to twenty-four," she tells me, "and whenever I go to the doctor, even for something completely unrelated, it's the first thing that they tell me. I had a series of really strong headaches and the first suggestion was 'I take control of the situation now,'" Jess says. "When I go to my appointment I say: 'I am not here to talk about my weight—I have struggled with disordered eating for fifteen years and I do not want to set off another relapse. If I decide to attempt to lose weight in the future, I will do so. Now: what can we do about my verruca?' I shouldn't have to do this. But it's better than coming away feeling ashamed and helpless."

Giving Birth

"When I'm in labor," I said to some friends recently, "I'm not going to let anyone put anything inside me before they've at least introduced themselves." Everyone around the table who had already given birth laughed, as if I'd announced that I would be having my baby removed by laser while someone gave me a head massage. This "oh you've got no idea" response has been typical anytime I express any opinion about labor or pregnancy as a childless woman. "That's not how it works," the friends at this dinner told me. "One nurse told me that I should pop my dignity by the door. I had people putting their hands in my vagina without even saying a word to me first," said another friend.

When I expressed horror at the idea of having someone put their hand inside my body without my consent, several of the women at the gathering seemed frustrated, telling me it's "not about how you feel, it's about getting a healthy baby." Apparently, I am unreasonable for thinking that it's a bit medieval that the options are either healthy baby or retaining some control over how you give birth.

In 2018, when Meghan Markle was pregnant with her first child, Archie, she came under lots of fire for wanting to give birth on her own terms. The first transgression came in the form of an announcement that she wouldn't be doing the post-birth photo shoot outside the hospital, à la Diana and Kate. Then it was the fact that she apparently passed over the traditional royal-birth medical team for a female doctor, saying that she didn't want her labor run by "men in suits" (I love you, Meghan).

For some reason, all of these perfectly reasonable choices made people furious. How dare the duchess try to choose how her baby was born? I'm not stupid. I, like most women, realize that labor isn't generally a fun experience, but is it really so unreasonable to expect decent treatment? Much of the commentary around Markle's birth focused on her being "ungrateful" for the top-tier care she had been offered. Critics went so far as to call her a "brat." But honestly, if being a "brat" is how you get full control of how you give birth, then sign me up.

It is shortsighted to discuss the way that Meghan Markle

is treated by the press and the general public without acknowledging the inherent racism she contends with every day. Would a white woman have been given quite such a hard time for wanting to choose her own birth plan?

We can't say for sure how much of Meghan Markle's treatment by the press during her pregnancy was due to racist stereotyping, but what we do know is that black women in the UK are five times more likely to die during childbirth than white women, so if anyone deserves to demand the highest possible standard of care, it is women of color.

Candice Brathwaite is a blogger and writer who nearly died of sepsis shortly after she gave birth to her daughter, despite having been reassured by medical professionals that she was "fine." She wrote an article for *Grazia Daily* in which she said: "Stories like mine are not unique. Recently A-list celebrities such as Beyoncé and Serena Williams have both spoken about their difficult births. Williams revealed that she had to argue her way into having a doctor examine her when she felt unwell after her C-section, even though she had a medical history of suffering from blood clots and was no doubt paying a pretty penny for her care." If these celebrities were treated this way, imagine what nonfamous women of color must deal with.

Brathwaite continues: "Having the data to hand made me braver about stating what I thought the issue had been all along and it was that the poor treatment was most definitely rooted in racial bias. From the moment I went to the doctor (who incorrectly assumed I was a single mother) up until during my induced labour when one of the midwives chastised me for not

being 'strong enough,' all of these microaggressions, judge-
ments and the flippant treatment were entirely down to the fact
that I was a black woman."

What Brathwaite hits on here is a tendency that many
women have to wait until we have insurmountable evidence
that we are right before we feel entitled to act. This is especially true for women who come from marginalized groups or
minorities, people who are used to being told that their experiences aren't real.

A word that was used to describe Meghan Markle a lot
during her pregnancy was "entitled." When she dismissed the
medical team because she didn't want her birth managed by
"men in suits," she was being selfish. When she (allegedly)
favored a home birth over the Lindo Wing, where Harry and
William were born, she was being spoiled. But here's the thing:
Meghan, like every other woman in the UK, was literally
entitled—entitled to choose how she gave birth.

Did you know that women are entitled to request elective
C-sections? Or that anxiety about giving birth is a legitimate
ground to have a planned C-section? I have read thread after
thread on the parenting website Mumsnet about how to "convince" your doctor to "allow" you to have a C-section, when in
the UK, and under the European Convention of Human Rights,
it is up to a woman how she chooses to give birth. Women also
have the right to refuse induction and to demand as much or as
little pain relief as is safe to take. It is the right kind of rude to say,
"I know I am entitled to do this the way I want to do it, please
help me to make the decision that is best for me and my baby."

Modern medicine is a marvel and it's something that we are very lucky to have access to, but medical staff are fallible—just like everyone else. It's easy to stop seeing patients as people and to forget that women's bodies during labor are still theirs—they aren't just birth machines. Our bodily autonomy doesn't stop during labor.

Whether it's a home birth or a scheduled C-section, you have a right to give birth the way that you want to, or at least to give it a go. If ever there is a time to discover the power of rude, it's during pregnancy. The system is old-fashioned and sees the only important outcome as you and your baby surviving. It's okay to want more than survival. It's okay to want to make plans and have those plans respected, just as it's okay to change your mind part of the way through. In no other grueling medical ordeal would you be expected to smile and act like you're lucky.

THE RIGHT KIND OF
Rude About Health

▶ Your health is one of the most precious resources that you have, so wanting to look after it is not unreasonable.

▶ Because health care is free in the UK, it can be harder to demand the standard of care that you require. However, medical professionals are still fallible, and therefore if you feel they are overlooking something important, you need to make that point until you feel heard.

▶ If you don't feel that medical staff are listening to you or treating you in a productive way, then you can and should change doctors.

▶ Taking data and evidence when you meet with your doctor can help them to understand that you require their help. This is especially valuable in terms of data around your menstrual cycle. There are dozens of apps that will allow you to chart this.

▶ Do not settle for a form of birth control that makes you feel unwell. Keep going back until you find something that works for you, or use condoms. There is nothing wrong with using protection only when you are actually having sex.

▶ Nothing about your body is wrong or gross. Illness is not a weakness or a fault, no matter how you contracted it. You deserve good-quality, effective medical care from a medical practitioner who treats you with kindness.

TALLULAH BANKHEAD

◂ ▸

Tallulah Brockman Bankhead (January 31, 1902–December 12, 1968) was an American stage and screen actress.

The Brockman Bandheads were a prominent Alabama political family. Tallulah's grandfather and uncle were both US senators, and her father served as a member of Congress. However, despite her family's conservative political affiliations, Tallulah publicly supported causes such as civil rights. She often openly opposed her own family, but that was only the beginning of her rude behavior.

Tallulah publicly displayed a healthy sexual appetite—not something that many women in her day and age were open about. She was unapologetically bisexual (though she preferred the term "ambisexterous") and was famous for having a lot of sex with both men and women. In 1932, during an interview with *Motion Picture*, she said: "I'm serious about love. I'm damned serious about it now . . . I haven't had an affair for six months. Six months! Too long . . . If there's anything the matter with me now, it's not Hollywood or Hollywood's state of mind . . . The matter with me is, I WANT A MAN! . . . Six months is a long, long while. I WANT A MAN!"

Following the release of the Kinsey Report (which explored human sexual orientation on a scale between 1 and 6), she commented, "I found no surprises in the Kinsey report. The good doctor's clinical notes were old hat to me . . . I've had many momentary love affairs. A lot of these impromptu romances have been climaxed in a fashion not generally condoned. I go into them impulsively. I scorn any notion of their permanence. I forget the fever associated with them when a new interest presents itself."

Perhaps the most appealing thing about Bankhead was her total lack of apology. In 1933 she nearly died following a five-hour emergency hysterectomy due to venereal disease. Only seventy pounds when she left the hospital, she stoically said to her doctor, "Don't think this has taught me a lesson!" Before the hysterectomy Bankhead had previously had four abortions, at a time when abortion was still technically illegal.

She died at age sixty-six due to double pneumonia, caused in part by her chain-smoking (Bankhead was said to smoke 150 cigarettes a day). Her last words were allegedly, "Codeine . . . bourbon."

Her unapologetic attitude toward her own health—and the fact that she prioritized the enjoyment of life over said health—should serve as a lesson to those of us who can't even bring ourselves to tell our GP how many of units of alcohol we drink each week. Bankhead didn't "mea culpa" for needing medical treatment as a result of living a passionate, sexual life. Instead she smiled through the consequences and lived life to the fullest.

Final Thoughts

The first thing I did when I started writing *Rude* was to keep a diary of my day, looking for times when my fear of rudeness reared its head. So, as I came to the end of the writing process, I decided to do it again in order to see how things had changed.

9:00 a.m.

I take the tube to work. On the platform, people try to push past me to get onto the train but I hold fast—not pushing back, but not letting them move me. When we get on the train, people are squashed by the doors even though there is space in the middle. Usually I would ignore the problem while silently seething with my face up against the glass. But today I move down, and to my surprise, other people follow me. I arrive at work without the sense of anger that always comes from Tube Wars.

9:35 a.m.

I am very slightly late for a meeting—only by a minute or two. I decide to take my own advice from the "Rude at Work" chapter and instead of piling into the meeting apologizing for my ineptitude, I sit down and say, "Thank you so much for waiting for me," and then we begin. It could just be my imagination, but it seems like people are listening more closely to my ideas.

11:00 a.m.

I go into another meeting to discuss an ongoing project. The person on the other side of the table wants me to put together a campaign with very little notice and no budget. I tell her that it's not really an option. In the past, I would have spent days trying to make it work and then would eventually have had to deliver the news that it wasn't possible. Instead, I am clear from the start. She is frustrated, but I leave the meeting knowing that I haven't made my own life more difficult and feel pleased.

1:00 p.m.

I'm so hungry that my concentration is slipping, and I need to eat. Someone asks if I can pop into a meeting for half an hour. "I need to eat something first," I say, overwhelmed by my own bravery. Traditionally I've just skipped lunch or drunk a Diet Coke and hoped that it would fill me up. Half an hour later I'm back at my desk with a renewed ability to concentrate. I join the end of the meeting and I'd like to think I'm quite helpful.

3:00 p.m.

I have to finish writing an article by four p.m., but one of my close friends who lives abroad is having problems. She sends me a stream of messages. Rather than go into a meeting room and WhatsApp her for as long as she needs and then turn in the article late, I channel my inner Melissa Fabello. I'm practically having heart palpitations as I send a message saying, "I'm just in the middle of something, can we chat later?" Her reply is a little terse, but I file the article on time.

5:00 p.m.
I get a message from some school friends about a bottomless brunch they want to go to. It costs $55 a head and it's all prosecco (which I don't like). I tell them that it's not my thing but that I'd love to see them soon, and amazingly other people start to agree. We all decide to skip the bottomless brunch but book a date for drinks in a few days' time.

5:30 p.m.
I have finished working, so without asking anyone I pack my things up. "I've been productive today," I say as I put my coat on. "See you all tomorrow."

7:00 p.m.
My husband comes home, and I suggest that as I've cooked all week, maybe he could pop some sausages in the oven and make some mashed potatoes. He's very happy to do so and even makes onion gravy. It's delicious and I tell him so. He tells me that he's really enjoying getting into cooking and that he previously assumed that I preferred to do the cooking, since, of the two of us, I know a bit more about how to cook. I realize that in my attempt to be a good partner, I've been putting great food on the table every night for the last six years, but I've

also been depriving him of the chance to enjoy learning to put meals together.

9:00 p.m.

I say I want to watch *Succession*, but my husband doesn't want to. He has a bath and reads in bed for a while. When I come to bed, he tells me that he likes this new routine we've fit into. "I like the fact that I never have to guess what you want or what you're thinking anymore," he tells me.

11:00 p.m.

Husband is snoring again—worse than ever. I decide to go and sleep in our spare room. It's hard to shake the feeling that we're failing at being married if we don't share a bedroom, but when the snoring is really bad, I need to sleep somewhere else. I've been doing it once or twice a week since I finished writing *Rude*, and in the morning, I wake up happier and more refreshed. Often I'll get up around six and go back to bed with him for a while, so that we still get to lie tangled up together before the alarm goes off.

Many times, in the course of writing this book, I worried that the examples I gave were too small or insignificant to mean much. But the thing about being afraid to be rude is that it doesn't ruin your life in a matter of days, weeks, or even months—it's death by a thousand tiny cuts. Every time someone pushes you and you don't say "Hey!," every time you apologize for something that isn't your fault, every time you put everyone else's wants and needs above your own, it builds up. And eventually your defining characteristic is that you try not to ever offend or annoy anyone around you.

The hallmarks of your life should be the things you do, not the things you avoid. An absence of something is not a goal. Attempting to live a life where you do not cause pain or harm to others is noble, but it's essential to do that while also attempting to live a life that makes you feel happy, valued, seen, and heard. Achieving that is a whole lot harder—perhaps even impossible—if you walk through the world terrified that people are going to think that you are rude.

I'll admit, though, that while writing this book has been more therapeutic than I ever anticipated, it has also been incredibly frustrating. The entire time I was writing, a voice at the back of my head kept saying, "Why should *we* have to change? Why should *we* have to be the ones who fix a world that is currently designed to fuck us over?" It doesn't seem right that we're indoctrinated into a cult of passivity and then expected to fight what has been ingrained in us since childhood. Of course, we shouldn't have to. Unfortunately, though, a lot of harnessing the power of rude is about accepting that the way things are and the way things should be are often not one and the same. Typically, your options are to complain about the system and to try to change it.

I'm far from the first person to conflate feminism and rudeness, and I'm not the first person to see an essential correlation between the two, but much of what I've read on the subject often seems to veer into the realm of victim-blaming. There are plenty of "feminists" who enjoy talking about how pathetic modern women have become, how we should learn to kick men in the balls rather than "letting" them push us into sex. I agree that women should try to embrace the power of rude, but I cannot tolerate the idea that it's somehow our fault if we can't. We shouldn't be held responsible for a message that was stamped into us from childhood.

The hardest part of writing this book was grappling with the fact that if you are able to start being a bit more positively rude, you may find yourself initially punished rather than rewarded. The rude way is almost always the hard way—at least at first.

If you finish this book and decide to stop saying yes when you mean no, turn down a bridesmaid role that you can't afford or don't want, demand a pay raise, or tell your boyfriend that you've been faking your orgasms for the last two years, I cannot pretend that it's going to go down well. The people in your life who are used to the old, deferential you may not be pleased. It might lead to arguments, breakups, friendship schisms, and work problems. People who used to call you sweet might stop doing so, and you need to ask yourself how you feel about that. Do you want to be "sweet"? Or do you want to do what you want when you want to do it?

Being rude doesn't have to be an all-or-nothing choice. You can pick and choose the moments to embrace the power of rude. You are not obligated to view rudeness like a religion. Rudeness is more like a superpower; it is something that you should deploy as and when you see fit.

Further Reading

All That Glitters: Anna Wintour, Tina Brown, and the Rivalry Inside America's Richest Media Empire by Thomas Maier

Be the Change: A Toolkit for the Activist in You by Gina Martin

The Favourite: Sarah, Duchess of Marlborough by Ophelia Field

How the Pill Changes Everything: Your Brain on Birth Control by Sarah E. Hill

Ma'am Darling: 99 Glimpses of Princess Margaret by Craig Brown

No One Is Too Small to Make a Difference by Greta Thunberg

Queen Bees and Wannabes: Helping Your Daughter Survive Cliques, Gossip, Boyfriends, and the New Realities of Girl World by Rosalind Wiseman

Rosa Parks: My Story by Rosa Parks with Jim Haskins

The Second Shift: Working Families and the Revolution at Home by Arlie Russell Hochschild

The Secret Diaries of Miss Anne Lister, vol. 1, *I Know My Own Heart* by Helena Whitbread

Tallulah: My Autobiography by Tallulah Bankhead

Why Men Earn More: The Startling Truth Behind the Pay Gap— and What Women Can Do About It by Dr. Warren Farrell

Acknowledgments

I rather flippantly dedicated *Rude* to myself, because I think it's fair to say that I did a lot of the heavy lifting on it. I share the dedication with my sister, who is the least rude woman I know. I remember sitting with her on a snowy February afternoon in Devon and telling her that I wanted to turn my experience of being a brief national news story into a work of practical nonfiction. We'd been kicking around other book ideas for as long as I could remember, but when I described the idea for this book, her face lit up: "That's the one," she told me. "You need to write that." So, I did. Thanks, Lucy.

Writing a book takes a lot more people than I had ever anticipated. First my amazing agent, Eve White, who has shepherded me through the whole process since I was a twenty-three-year-old student, alongside Ludo Cinelli. Then the entire team at Trapeze, who welcomed me as a new author writing nonfiction for the first time, and Carina Guiterman, who gave the US version of *Rude* such a brilliant edit.

I also need to thank the entire early pregnancy unit team at the Elizabeth Garrett Anderson wing of University College

London Hospital, who looked after me with such compassion during some of the darkest days of my life.

I promised that if my mortgage advisor, David Hutchinson, managed to get my mortgage approved, I'd mention him here. You're a wizard, David. Thank you for the home.

I'd also like to thank Layla, Ivy, and Erin, respectively three years old, two and a half years old, and ten months old at the time of writing. When I thought about my hope for this book, it was that you three never make the same choices that I did, or at least that you make them by desire rather than obligation.

Then, of course, the list of people who kept me sane and listened to me complain bitterly about trying to write a book while having a full-time job: Tim, Charlotte, Lucy, George, Flick, Hannah C., Steph, Ieuan, Aimee, Georgie, Carol, Rebecca and Felix, Ian, Katie, Rob, Natalie, Ed, Juliette, Madeleine, Graham, Natalie, Rob, Liv, Grace, Kathy, Emily, Mel, Chloe, Pete, Emma, Jon, Ellen, Miranda, Jess, Lisa, Faima, Luke, Pavlina, Tessy, and Dinah.

Last, of course, my husband, Marcus, who pours the wine, wipes the tears, takes my ASOS returns to the post office, and never gets cross when I invite twelve people to an impromptu dinner. I love you. Thank you for choosing such a rude wife.

About the Author

Rebecca Reid is a twentysomething freelance writer. Her novels include *Perfect Liars* and *The Truth Hurts*. Rude is her first work of nonfiction. When she's not writing books, Rebecca spends her time writing screenplays, having debates on the television, and baking cookies (though rarely all at the same time). She lives in London with her husband.